TEACHERS TALK

ESTELLE FUCHS is an anthropologist and associate professor of education at Hunter College of the City University of New York. She is author of *Pickets at the Gates* and completed *Teachers Talk* in conjunction with her work as a member of Project TRUE at Hunter College.

Teachers Talk

Views from Inside City Schools

BY ESTELLE FUCHS

Anchor Books
Doubleday & Company, Inc.
Garden City, New York

Sponsored by a training grant from the office of Juvenile Delinquency and Youth Development, Welfare Administration, U. S. Department of Health, Education and Welfare in co-operation with the President's Committee on Juvenile Delinquency and Youth Crime.

The Anchor Books edition is the
first publication of *Teachers Talk*

Anchor Books edition: 1969

Library of Congress Catalog Card Number 69-13701
Copyright © 1967, 1969 by Estelle Fuchs
All Rights Reserved
Printed in the United States of America

LC
5133
.N4
F8
1969

The data for the cases in this book were originally compiled under the auspices of Project TRUE (Teacher Resources for Urban Education). Project TRUE was sponsored by Grant Numbers 64227, 65230, and 66228, Office of Juvenile Delinquency and Youth Development, and by the Department of Education, Hunter College, City University of New York, 1963–67.

The author is indebted to Dr. Marjorie B. Smiley, Director of Project TRUE, for her careful and constructive reading of the manuscript, and to Dr. Elizabeth M. Eddy, Director of Research, Project TRUE, and Mrs. Helen Randolph for their assistance.

Grateful acknowledgment goes to Mr. Norman Bailey, Miss Helene Siegel, Miss Carol Bryant, Mr. Charles Haseloff, for their assistance in preparing the manuscript.

Special thanks go to all the beginning teachers who participated in the Project TRUE research by carefully airing their ongoing school experiences. It is hoped that their experiences, sometimes painful, always poignant, will pave the way for more constructive experiences for those who follow in their path.

Estelle Fuchs, Ph.D.
Hunter College
The City University of New York

TABLE OF CONTENTS

	PREFACE	v
	INTRODUCTION	ix
I:	**EUPHORIA OR THE HONEYMOON PERIOD**	
	1. The First Day	3
II:	**PANIC OR THE FALL**	
	2. Culture Shock	17
	3. Machismo: Culture Conflict in the Classroom	27
	4. The Escalator	38
	5. Soap Doesn't Always Clean	46
	6. The Dumping Ground	60
	7. Fatigue: The Lesson Plan	73
III:	**HELP!**	
	8. The Rexograph Machine	79
	9. Bypassed or the Art Lesson	96
	10. "We Know Better" or Grouping	102
	11. Exploited	113
	12. Who Stole the Cookie Money?	124
	13. Parents	131
IV:	**ADJUSTING**	
	14. The Observation: A *Rite de Passage*	143
	15. Getting Help	164
	16. The Saga of Class 1/5	172

17. The Christmas Party: A Rite of Intensification	185
18. School Boycott	199
POSTSCRIPT	213
INDEX	217

INTRODUCTION

Teachers Talk is written to provide insights into the concerns and needs of neophyte teachers in inner-city schools. It is based on materials gathered by Project TRUE (Teacher Resources for Urban Education), a research and curriculum development project carried on by the Department of Education, Hunter College, City University of New York, between 1963–67.

As part of the research endeavor, a sample of the graduates of the education program who were in their first semester of teaching in inner-city elementary schools were invited to record their experiences. Each Saturday morning during their first semester, fourteen of the teachers who had been assigned to "special service" schools, i.e., schools in deprived areas of the city, with high minority group populations, reading retardation, and conditions generally considered "difficult," described their experiences in intensive, taped interviews. They responded in detail to questions concerning lessons; interaction with pupils, teachers, supervisors, and parents; reactions to school regulations; curriculum materials; and other professionally relevant social issues such as strikes and school boycotts.

The data collected represent a wealth of information about daily life in inner-city classrooms and schools as perceived by beginning teachers, and provide valuable insights into the critical period of teacher induction as members of ghetto school staffs.

Teachers Talk is organized around a series of impressions and concerns expressed by the teachers as they moved through their first semester. They include the teacher's first day, problems concerning discipline, classroom observations by supervisors, the seeking and finding of professional help, relations with parents, extra-class duties, and the general area of "human relations."

In each section of the book a series of anecdotes taken directly from the taped teacher accounts is presented, followed by a brief discussion. Although the anecdotes represent a small fraction of the voluminous accounts collected by Project TRUE, they are dramatic illustrations of experiences commonly faced by beginning teachers in similar schools. Names have been altered to protect the privacy of the individuals and schools involved, and a minimum of editing was done for the sake of clarity.

The discussions of the incidents are based upon relevant social science theory, with an emphasis upon theory contributed by cultural anthropology. Until relatively recently, anthropological insights concerning school behavior have been almost completely absent from education literature. It is true that studies of social class and its influence upon behavior and learning have drawn upon anthropological concepts and methods. On the whole, however, of the behavioral sciences, educational psychology and to a lesser extent sociology have been the major contributors to American educational thought. The anthropologist recognizes the validity of these and other disciplines. Yet anthropology has unique contributions to make toward the development of insights. The relative absence of this contribution rests largely with the dearth of professional anthropologists concerned with research in American education. Increasingly, however, anthropologists are turning their attention to problems of American culture and the area of education is one which is witnessing active interest.

What is it that anthropology especially offers to the education of teachers and administrators? The most significant contribution is that of developing cultural awareness. George Spindler has stated this clearly:

. . . The aim is to create in the teacher an awareness of how his culture influences specifically what he does as a teacher and how his students' culture influences what they do, and how to think about, observe, and analyze these influences. Cultural awareness as one goal is particularly important for the administrator, since he manipulates the setting in which the teacher interacts with students and parents. He must not only display cultural awareness but must also understand the mechanics of culture change, the cultural expectations affecting the leader's role, the concrete as well as idealistic meaning of cultural values, and the social system of the school in the setting of the encompassing community and national social structure. . . .[1]

That anthropological insights and methods, as well as subject content, have a great deal to offer school personnel is being increasingly recognized in professional circles across the nation, among both anthropologists and educators. Educators today must deal with myriad problems including those emanating from accelerated automation, population growth, a knowledge explosion, rapid urbanization, and civil rights revolution. In our society, where values, beliefs, and attitudes are undergoing rapid change, understanding of cultural patterns and social pressures as they affect the schools and the people working in them have become essential. A deeper understanding of the role of education in the cultural process as well as understandings and techniques for effective functioning by educators are among the contributions anthropology can make. Among other things, the theoretical insights and techniques of anthropology offer educators sharpened awareness of the community context of the school, the significance of conflict between cultural ideals and realities, the problems of ethnic, race, and class relations as they affect education, and educational and cultural forces as they affect the developing child. To these problems the anthropologist brings the perspective of a world view which comes from

---

[1] George D. Spindler, "Anthropology and Education: An Overview," in George D. Spindler, *Education and Culture*, New York: Holt, Rinehart & Winston, 1963, pp. 65–66.

his experience with other people and cultures, and a deep awareness that the child brings a great deal with him when he enters the school setting—that he comes not as a *tabula rasa*, but rather as an active participant in the educative process.

Educational failure in the inner city is of particular concern in American education today and inseparable from major economic, political, and social issues confronting the nation. The search for the improvement of the education of children is bound up with efforts to improve the quality of the teaching they receive. In the search for improved quality a study of beginning teachers has great relevance. One reason for this is that the teaching ranks are likely to continue in the future to contain large numbers of neophytes. Another is that increased knowledge of the beginners' experiences can provide insights concerning the forces that make teachers function as they do.

One of the major criticisms leveled against the "slum" school or inner-city school has been that it contains large numbers of inexperienced teachers. Indeed, so great has been the concern over this fact that deliberate efforts to create staff stability and a favorable index of experienced to inexperienced teachers are a primary concern for principals, Boards of Education, and community groups.

It would seem that, although staff stability may very well be desirable, staff transiency and teacher inexperience are not only characteristic of inner-city schools, but must ever be regarded as an ordinary condition—a canceled-out factor as it were. The general transiency of the American population both as regards employment and residence has affected school staffs. Even with a decline in the problem of attracting teachers to work in inner-city schools, it seems unrealistic to anticipate that teachers will stay the number of years which, in other times and places, enable them to have long-term acquaintance with families of their children and with the neighborhood. And, indeed, neither do teachers stay the number of years to permit neighborhood traditions and gossip passed down from sibling to sibling to develop about them.

Several factors account for this projection of teacher turnover as a constant. One is that young female teachers marry (or hope to); young male teachers seek advancement out of the classroom. Young women follow their husbands, who often find employment away from the city. The teachers are of child-bearing age. The nuclear family and the disappearance of the nursemaid and housekeeper class to serve the lower middle-class teacher's household combine to keep young teachers at home during the early years of child-rearing. The distance she must travel from residence out of the inner city, sometimes from outlying suburbs, makes it difficult for many women to remain on the inner-city school staff. All these factors, and others, serve to increase teacher mobility. Even the older woman, returning after rearing her children, tends to seek employment in schools more conveniently located to her own place of residence and presenting fewer problems. Economic conditions and other factors in the larger society may alter the picture, as may arrangements for part-time teaching programs for experienced personnel. Recruitment of staff from ghetto communities and recruitment of well-meaning, enthusiastic young Americans coming from the Peace Corps, VISTA, and social service traditions is a likelihood in the future.

In itself, changed recruitment of personnel is not enough to change teaching in the inner city. Teachers do not work in a vacuum. They are, very early in their careers, inducted into the ongoing social system of the school in which they work. Some teachers bring with them a special charisma that enables them to achieve great educative results despite overwhelming obstacles. These are the "naturals." Unfortunately, for most the real picture is different, for teachers, after all, are quite human, and charisma is rare indeed. All supervisors can point with pride and relief to superb teachers within their schools. No supervisor with any sense of reality can assume that all his teachers are masters nor can he assume that they do not need help. They do. They will continue to need assistance for many reasons. Teachers themselves recognize this. To the inexperienced teacher assistance is particularly urgent. Even the briefest stay ought to be a constructive educational experience for teacher and pupil alike.

Whether or not there is professional growth and constructive teaching rather than disaster in the form of educational failure for inner-city children is related not merely to the teacher's control over traditional methodology, as important as that is, but also to the institutional context of the school itself and the pressure it exerts upon the people within it.

This book is written to provide insights into the problems of beginning teachers as they are experienced within the institutional setting of the large inner-city school. It is written for prospective teachers, beginners, administrators, and all others concerned with improving the education of children and their teachers.

PART I

EUPHORIA OR THE HONEYMOON PERIOD

CHAPTER 1

The First Day

The first day is exceptional in that it generally proceeds relatively smoothly and is characterized by the excitement, thrill, and general state of euphoria which accompanies the beginning of the school year. There are traces of apprehension as well. Here are descriptions of the first meetings between beginning teachers and their pupils, before the apprehension grows in significance and develops into a state of panic.

Miss Winters
Grade 2/4[1]

September 14. The best thing that happened to me on the first day was that at 2:30 one little boy raised his hand and said that he was happy that he was in my class. Afterward, many other children raised their hands and said they also liked being in my class. I asked them why and they said it was because they knew that in my class they were going to learn.

---

[1] Large city schools usually have several classes on a single grade level. The first number refers to the grade, the second exponent refers to the number of the particular class. Thus 2/4 refers to the second grade, class number 4. Sometimes, although not necessarily, the classes on a grade are arranged hierarchically and the exponent is a clue to whether or not a class is considered "good" or "poor." Almost all the teachers reporting here were assigned middle classes on the grade.

This made me feel very happy. I didn't want them to feel that they were in my class just because the principal put them there. They thought that they were in my class to learn and I was going to teach them.

Miss Hanes
Grade 3/4

September 14. I think the most important thing that happened was during the first few minutes of my class. I had spent quite a bit of time before my first day thinking about what it would be like and I had anticipated the worst. I worried about what would happen if I were unable to control my class. Would my teaching be effective? I just really didn't know what to expect.

I picked up my class in the yard and marched them up to the classroom and began the routines that I had planned for the first few minutes of class. I began with the seating arrangement and everything seemed to work out fine. Actually, after I got started, everything was just wonderful! I felt so good I couldn't believe it was happening. I had expected bedlam.

My first day in class turned out to be a very good and productive one. I think that most of the things that happened to me were really unexpected. I hadn't felt very sure of myself and I had not expected to do as well as I did.

One of the unexpected things was the size of my class. I had expected twenty-six children on my register. When I got there, there were only eighteen children present. I knew that many of them would be coming late and perhaps be delayed a day or two. I felt, however, that I could set up the routines that I had planned even though I knew that I would have to be going over them. I felt a little disturbed at first but I thought I might just as well go ahead and then repeat them as I would be repeating them many times anyway—probably every time a new child came into the room.

During the day I received a steady stream of new admissions. This was also something I had not expected. I had expected that my class would all be there and stay there all day. Even up until a few minutes before 3:00, however, I was receiving children into my room from other classes. Each

The First Day

time a child came in I had to introduce myself again. It was usually, of course, right in the middle of a lesson and I had to stop, acquaint the child with what we were doing, and see if he could pick it up from there. Besides that, I would have to show him where to hang up his clothes, find him a seat, give him paper, etc. This didn't, however, prove disrupting at all, which surprised me.

Another thing which I had not expected was that all the children came to school as prepared as they did. I had spent some time in the school student-teaching and substitute-teaching and I remembered that the teachers had to drill and drill to get the children to come to school prepared, to come on time, to bring a notebook and a pencil. I remembered being in a class where every day ten children would come in without any pencils or notebooks. Fortunately everyone in my class came very prepared. Everyone was there on time and those who were not had been admitted late. They all brought pencils and notebooks and seemed eager to get started.

The thing that surprised me most was that I did as much actual teaching as I did. I had thought so much about routines for the first day and I really had to spend very little time on them. The children, of course, are in the third grade and had been in the school for at least two years—many of them for three—so they were acquainted with the classroom routine. I don't suppose that they differ very much from class to class—the method of hanging up clothing, the method of putting away books, taking out books, lining up, etc. These are routines which are set down by the school. I found that most of the children in my class had been very well trained by their former teachers and were acquainted with the routines and followed them well. I had to go through most of the routines only once or twice with a few corrections to those individuals who were not doing them properly. I began to realize that I would go over routines every day as we got to them, emphasizing them for the first, maybe, two months. After that, when they had become more or less second nature, I wouldn't have to do so much with them.

On the whole, and contrary to my expectations, I found the children in my class to be very alert and attentive. On the first day back from the summer vacation I had heard from other teachers that they would be very restless, but they weren't. They were very alert. There were one or two, of course, who were unattentive, but on the whole the class was bright and alert.

Another surprise was that the first day went very quickly. I thought it would just drag. I felt that half the day I would be at a loss as to what to do and it would really be a very long day. Yet before I knew it the day was over. It went very, very quickly. Actually very few of the things that I did expect happened to me. I thought from my student-teaching experience here and my days of substitute-teaching that I knew a great deal about my school. I thought I knew exactly what to expect and found that I didn't at all.

One thing, however, that did happen and that I did expect was a fire drill. At a meeting the previous week the principal had announced that there would be a fire drill, and I was prepared for it. I had planned and did teach a lesson on the importance of the fire drill with an experience chart. We discussed safety rules during a fire drill, why they are important and why they are to be followed. We practiced the routine of lining up, getting our clothing, and doing everything quickly and quietly; and actually going up and down the stairs, showing them the exit which we would use, so that it went very well.

I think that the very best thing that happened to me the first day of school was the feeling of self-assurance that I got being there. It's hard to describe exactly how this happened. I'm not sure I even know exactly how it did happen. But after I had been in front of the room for a few minutes and I saw that things were going so well, I suddenly felt that I was doing very well for a beginning teacher, that things would work out fine in the future.

I really can't think of anything at all that happened to me on the first day that I could classify as worst, because nothing really terrible happened. I had some minor discipline problems which I had expected, things like speaking in class to your neighbor and speaking on line. I assume that this happens in every class, no matter how experienced the teacher, and they are things which happen in the normal course of

The First Day

events with which one has to deal. I wouldn't consider these "worst" as they didn't present any great problem.

At the end of my first school day, I really felt wonderful and this is the most unexpected of all! I had expected to go home, exhausted and worn out. I think this was mainly a result of my substitute-teaching experience. In my last term of college I had two free days every week and I spent quite a few of them doing substitute-teaching at three or four schools in the general area of my school and in the school that I am in now. I used to come home very discouraged and worn out and exhausted. Of course, I guess I didn't take into full consideration the fact that a substitute teacher is not on the same working basis as a regular teacher, that the children tend to take advantage of a substitute teacher. I knew at the end of the first day that I was going to enjoy teaching and I felt that, once I got used to everything and became really familiar with all the teaching techniques, things would be really great.

I felt very good about the school the first day. Everyone had been extremely helpful. They kept asking me how things were going and really encouraging me. Lunch with the other new teachers was one of the best experiences of the day. The minute we got together we started talking about things that had happened, funny experiences, and we had a good laugh; and I felt very good about the children whom I would be teaching. I knew that they were not a particularly bright group. All of them were reading below their reading levels, some of them very far below. I knew that I would have many problems, scholastic problems, with them, but they are a very responsive group on the whole and they seemed to be very willing. I felt very good about the thought of working with them for the whole year.

**Miss Samson
Grade 4/2**

September 14. My first day of school I went down and I brought my class up from the yard. Everybody was very quiet. I really thought that this was going to be one of the best classes that I had ever seen. Then, of course, I realized that this was the first day of school and everybody was on his guard, his best behavior. This was a strange situation.

I brought them upstairs and I showed them how we were going to line up to come into the room. I assigned seats. I made a temporary seating plan so that I could call the children by name. (This is very important and it adds to their respect for you as a teacher. We had discussed this at our orientation conference and I found it to be very effective when you call a child by name instead of pointing at him.) Then I established class routines: how we would put away our clothing; how we would get our clothing; raising your hand when you have something to say, not calling out; not talking when I'm talking; not talking when I haven't given permission to talk; not talking when you are doing something. I told them that we would have free time for talking. Then we discussed fire drills, what we would do and how we would line up, and our behavior in the hall and in the yard. I also covered supplies, the things that I requested that they bring in, and any problems. I complimented them on how they were dressed and how I would like them to come to school from now on, dressed neatly and clean; we discussed routines at home, the time we go to bed at night, how we take our bath, what happens when you get up in the morning. We discussed why breakfast is called breakfast and why we eat breakfast. Before we knew it the whole morning had gone and it had been a very good morning.

I felt that the children were not disappointed or hostile toward me even though I had held them in place in line. I think they were glad of that.

In the afternoon we reviewed some of the things that we had discussed in the morning as far as routine went, and I assigned a composition to tell me what they had done during the summer so I could get a look at their writing and their level. I found there was a great deal of regression over the summer.

I don't think there was anything unexpected that happened on my first day. I think everything went fairly much as I expected. I knew my class was going to be very well behaved on the first day because most children in that type of situation would behave. I saw no immediate difficulties. Everything

The First Day

went as I had expected. There was no outstanding thing. They behaved. They talked. We raised our hands. They got up and it went off pretty smoothly. There was no great problem.

At the end of my first day I was really thrilled with teaching. I enjoyed it immensely and I was very encouraged with my class and with potential that I saw. I was discouraged with my classroom, and had been since last week, because I haven't got anything. I can't start to actually fix it up and it happens to be a very dingy-looking room, a very dirty classroom. I have to take care of that. We started to clean it and decorate it but it will take time. Other than that, as far as my class is concerned, I was encouraged and was very enthusiastic after the first day.

Miss Brewster
Grade 2/3

September 14. Actually, I felt that everything that happened was very important for me as well as for the children. Getting them set in their routines, starting work, getting them used to writing in their notebooks, giving orders to them to do certain things was very important to me. I really felt very good giving them these orders and telling them what to do. Now I had the power position for once!

The best thing that happened to me on the first day was being such a tyrant and not showing that I was a softie right away. I figured while I was sitting there that the children were probably hating me but I wasn't taking it to heart because I wanted to get them straight right away on what I expected of them and not let them take advantage of me.

At 3:00 o'clock I said, "Good afternoon, class," and waited for their reply. As we walked out of the door everyone ran over and started to kiss me, which I let them do the first day because I couldn't help it. They all surrounded me. This sort of made me feel very good, knowing that I really didn't let them get away with anything and getting the satisfaction that these children would co-operate. It was a very good feeling that is hard to explain, having all the children run over to me; but I decided that it really can't go on all the time because every day the children just don't run over and kiss the teacher, and really get personal with her. We were told at our meetings the week before that we really shouldn't take this too personally because when you get too involved with any child it's hard to pass judgment or do anything with him.

Actually, nothing really bad happened the first day. As I said, everything was just fine. The children did whatever I said and no one talked back to me. In fact, I found throughout the week that if I were to say something to the effect that I didn't like what they were doing, they would just not do it and I would get no fresh answers. They listened and did what they were told. Of course, a few minutes later they would forget, but it's hard to expect too much of them because they are only in the second grade. I know when I sat in a class I still talked, so how can I expect my class to be quiet when I talk and they are learning?

How did I feel about teaching at the end of the first day? I really enjoyed it. I was very exhausted, which I have found to be true every day of the week, just coming home and feeling very tired. But I really enjoyed the feeling that I was helping these children, especially when they could answer me and the answers were correct. They really knew what they were doing and they enjoyed it. I could see it in their faces and in their answers—the way they raised hands eager to answer and jumped out of their seats all the time. I really enjoyed teaching. I was really looking forward to coming back the next day. I couldn't wait to get home and plan new things, make up signs, and bring in the next day's routines to go through in the morning.

As far as the school itself, it was very friendly. I went up to the teachers' lunchroom and ate lunch. The teachers were very friendly. They had told the new teachers to bring cups for coffee and they would boil the water. We hadn't brought anything the first day but they told us that we should come up anyway and they would give us coffee. They also told us that if we needed any help to please come and ask.

The First Day

**Miss Harris
Class 2/6**

September 14. The entire week was a new experience and therefore everything was important. Probably the most outstanding event was meeting my class for the first time and finding out that the plans I had made for them were utterly useless because of the lack of any previous training. The scholastic rating of the class is far below that required for a second grade. Most of the children were only doing kindergarten work, reading level, reading readiness, or pre-primer. I found that I had difficulty figuring out what to give the children to cope with this and I found it difficult to give any copy work because the children did not know the formation of letters. I could not ask them to give an idea of what they had learned because many of them did not recognize their own names. There were many discipline problems which caused the entire class to be disrupted. Several of the children are under guidance counseling and I am hoping to have them removed from the class.

The first day in class began by meeting the children in the basement of the school. The children had to locate their lines by looking for a card which had the name of their class, 2/6, and the room, 302. However, the second classroom had been changed and therefore my line was meeting with the first grades, which did cause a bit of chaos because most of these first-grade classes came to my line. I was in the place of a 1/7 class which was at that point located with the second grade. Because of this I have three children in my class who do not belong, who could not find their lines and do not know the name of their class. We are trying to relocate these children at this point. When we went to the room and the children were seated I discovered that eight of my children were not present.

Before school started, our orientation leader told us that the first thing to do was to see that the children learned the heading for the paper and then we could progress with other work. I had planned my lesson on how to introduce the heading; the papers were to be given out and the children were to be told who the monitors were going to be. However, after giving out the paper I discovered that the majority of my children could not write. They could not form letters. Several of the children had been sent from N.E. classes, i.e., completely non-English-speaking classes, and did not even recognize their names. Therefore the entire lesson went to pieces. Some of the children would not co-operate, tore up their papers, ran around the room. I discovered at this point who my guidance problem children were. I had read their records and had noticed the behavioral patterns and at this point knew who these children were. Because the supply lists were not to be collected until Wednesday, this room had very few supplies. I had planned on having the children draw some of their summer experiences and therefore help me to decorate the room. However, we did not have the crayons. We tried to do this with pencils but of course it was not as successful as working with the color media. I told the children that I was to have their names and addresses the next day and this was to be their homework assignment. I wrote it on the board. However, they could not copy it. Therefore I had to write individual notes for each child to take home. This was to be the homework assignment and in addition each child was to bring his two pencils and a notebook.

Having substituted in the school to which I am now appointed, I felt that I knew somewhat of the discipline problems in the school. However, I felt that with their own teacher there would be a bit more respect, knowing that this teacher could resort to calling upon parents. However, the most unexpected thing that happened to me was to realize that this had very little impression upon the children. At the end of the day I was completely exhausted and rather discouraged because of the lack of the use of planning which I had spent many hours doing, the lack of supplies which I could not draw upon, and finding that my plans were of no use. I felt that the children had little preparation for the second grade and that many of them were not emotionally ready for this class. This was because of the many social-behavioral disturbances which had caused those that were able to cope with the second-grade atmosphere and work to be completely held back. The first day there were nineteen children in attendance.

Eight children were absent. Of the nineteen, two did not belong in the room. In the afternoon, an additional girl arrived, who was for a 2/8 rather than a 2/6 class. However, she remained in the room because she did not know what her last name was. The next day I discovered that she was a brain-damaged child and was unable to locate her own teacher.

DISCUSSION

"This is it! You're in it and this is what you wanted!" is the way one beginning teacher described her first meeting with the children in her class. On the whole, the initial confrontation with their classes expressed by beginning teachers conjures up the excitement, thrill, and general state of euphoria which accompanies the beginning of the school year. There are traces of apprehension as well, and it does not take very long before apprehension grows in significance and develops into a state of panic.

The first day, however, is exceptional in that it usually proceeds relatively smoothly with the teacher and the children both on "best behavior," sizing one another up—a calm before the impending storm.

For the teacher, the major concern appears to establishing authority over the children. They are surprised that their inner-city, depressed-area pupils not only look normal, appear appropriately clothed for school, have come prepared for the business of learning with pencil, papers, but also that they speak English. The teacher tends to spend most of the time "establishing routines," letting the children know who is "boss," and laying down the rules. There is evidence of some fear and suspicion of the children on the teacher's part, based on hearsay.

There is, surprisingly, little in the way of welcome for the children. These teachers, young and inexperienced, act out what they believe to be appropriate evidence of a stern version of their new status—the teacher. Obviously insecure, the teacher sees the children's behavior as a test of whether or not she is adequately fulfilling the teacher role. Since most of the children behave at the beginning, they appear to be giving evidence to the teacher that she is successful. Thus the first day usually passes happily and quickly.

On the other hand, not all teachers experience euphoria, or the honeymoon period. When the children do not act according to the expectations of the teacher, she is sorely disappointed and prone to blame the youngsters for all that goes wrong. Thus Miss Harris does not appear to realize that the fact that the children cannot write their names can become the basis for a lesson in which she prepares name tags and helps them with their letters. The fact that the children are unable to respond to her preconceived notion of what they should be able to do is not seen as the basis of instruction. That her prearranged lesson plan is useless is upsetting to her, and although she is aware of all the deficiencies in the preparation of supplies, orderly welcome for the new class, etc., she nonetheless suggests that it is the children's fault that so many things went wrong.

That this teacher may very well have been assigned an exceptionally difficult class is true. The fact that she had been a substitute teacher in the same school where she was assigned as a regular teacher may have marked her as an "experienced" beginner, and thus likely to get a more difficult class than newly assigned teachers, who tend to get classes in the middle range of the grade—not the brightest, not the slowest. Nonetheless, her disappointment in the class and her lack of preparation for it provides an inauspicious beginning of the school year for the children, many of whom are already branded as "guidance cases."

However, for most teachers, the first day gives few clues to the problems of the future. The obedience and orderliness experienced by most of the beginning teachers during the first days are not long in disappearing. Quite rapidly, in a matter of days or weeks, a sense of panic develops in many teachers. Why doesn't the "good" feeling, the mutual "respect" persist? What happens to destroy the relative calm of the beginning?

Following are incidents that describe and discuss some of the "panic" reactions as they set in for the teacher during the first year.

PART II

PANIC OR THE FALL

CHAPTER 2

Culture Shock

The first few weeks in a school represent a dangerous period for the beginner. Fatigue, discipline problems, and self-doubt appear typical. Early in this critical period the new teacher exhibits symptoms of what anthropologists term "culture shock."

Mrs. Bender
Grade 5/2

October 5. There are two ways of looking at the most important thing that happened this week in school: a positive and a negative. As a positive way, Bobby, my "friend," has been taken from my class. He was transferred to a 5/4 class.

From the beginning of the term I have had discipline problems with him. I didn't call his mother because she was in the hospital having a baby. I don't know who the father is; I don't believe she does either. Anyway, I haven't been able to contact her. I did, however, speak to the guidance counselor, Mrs. Rogers, about him, and she's been watching him for a while. She's started a file on him but I haven't seen it yet.

Tuesday was an impossible day for me. I just didn't know what I was going to do with him. *I came home. I was hysterical. I cried all afternoon, all evening, and all night. I really felt that this was the end. I was not going back and what was the sense of knocking myself out? It wasn't worth it. Here I was trying to help people. They don't want to accept you and this is exactly what I felt, very useless* [author's emphasis]. I felt that I was not a teacher; I was a policeman. What did I need this aggravation for?

Wednesday, everything was fine. The class was marvelous. There was no problem.

Thursday, again, because of Bobby, everything went wrong. He had stolen . . . well, I didn't actually see him and couldn't accuse him . . . but paper clips were missing from my desk and while we were going up the stairs at lunchtime Bobby was throwing paper clips at the other children. I was afraid that one of these clips would end up in someone's eye. But, too, it was just one of those things. Everything that he did really got under my skin. I'd gotten to the point where I just wanted to take him and throw him down the flight of stairs we were on. He was just impossible!

On that same day, Mrs. Rogers, the guidance counselor, passed by my room to observe Bobby. He was in his seat so she just really couldn't understand what my fussing was all about. It just so happened that when she came in, he was in his seat taking a diagnostic test in math that I had prepared. She questioned me as to what was wrong and why I was so upset. I explained exactly what he was doing and told her that I just couldn't take it any more. "It's either him or me. I won't continue this way any more," I said, "because I'm becoming a manic-depressive. Monday, I go home; I'm fine. The next day I'm just very, very upset. I can't deal with my feelings any more." Well, she sent me out of the room and said that I should take a rest. She said she felt that I was very upset. She knew it! I'm sure she could see it!

I went down to the office to rexograph some stencils I had prepared and the principal walked in. All he had to do was say something nice to me! And that's exactly what he did. He said, "Well, Mrs. Bender, how is it going?"

I just started to cry. I could not control my feelings. I couldn't control anything. He asked what the problem was and all I had to say was, "Bobby."

"Is it just Bobby?" he said.

"Yes, it's just Bobby."

He said, "Well, if this is truly the problem, Bobby will be taken out of your class tomorrow. There is no need for you

Culture Shock

to feel so upset about it." Then he sort of scolded me, saying, "Why didn't you come to me before and tell me about this? Don't let things go so far. You are a human being; you have feelings. This isn't the way to react."

Now I was so upset that I just wanted to be left alone. I didn't want him to come near me. I didn't even want to go back to the classroom. I just wanted to go home.

I did go back to the classroom, however, and handed out the stencils I had run off and we did a music lesson. But my heart wasn't really in it because I felt that I was never going to come back. What's the sense?

Later I discussed this with my parents and my husband and with my contemporaries in the school. We all decided . . . well, I decided actually that the best thing would be for Bobby to get out of my class. Friday, yesterday, when I walked into the room the guidance counselor informed me that Bobby would be taken out of my class as of that day. And yesterday the class was a class. I was a teacher! I wasn't a baby-sitter; I wasn't a disciplinarian. I was a teacher. I had prepared lessons; I had done my lessons; I had completed what I planned. This was the first time that this had ever happened and I felt that this was the most important thing that happened to me in the school—never mind the week!—in the school so far.

In a negative way another important thing happened to me in school this week. There is a girl in my class (her name is Jean), a tall Negro girl who is constantly talking. I'm constantly reprimanding her for talking in class and in the hallways. Well, coming up from the assembly this week, Jean was hiding behind another girl, another Negro girl, and she was talking. I happened to catch her and I said to her, "Jean, I can see you." Well, Jean broke out in a rage. She started to cry and I couldn't imagine what was wrong. I thought perhaps she wasn't feeling well. She walked into the classroom. She was still crying with her head down on the desk. I went over to her and said, "Jean, what's wrong? Tell me and I'll help you if I can."

She wouldn't answer me but a few minutes later Bobby delivered a note to me from Jean. The note said, "Mrs. Bender, do you think my face is too black? Just let me know."

I became hysterical. I couldn't imagine what this was all about. So I asked her to stay with me during lunch and explain what she was talking about.

She did stay but she just couldn't answer me. I kept asking her questions. I told her I was her friend; I was her teacher; I was not there to hurt her, I was there to teach her. I don't know if it penetrated or not. She just stood there looking at me. I just couldn't make her out. She just stared at me with her eyes opened wide and she looked away from me. It was just like nothing, absolutely nothing.

Then, on Thursday, I also discussed the matter with her. I had a special conference with her and I wanted to know why she continued to disturb the class and talk. Well, in the course of our conversation, she said, "Well, why do you keep only the Negro kids in and let the Puerto Ricans go home? You don't like us, do you?"

Again, I was very upset because this was, of course, a lie and I told her so. I told her, "Jean, you know the people who stay and you name them for me." She named about seven Negro children.

I said, "But, Jean, you're not telling everything. There are more people that I keep in. You know that as well as I do. So go ahead and name everyone."

She proceeded to name the Puerto Rican children.

I asked her, "Jean, why did you say this to me if you know that I'm not being partial to one group? I don't understand how you reason."

Well, she didn't answer me but from then on everything seemed to go smoothly with her. She's my pal now, and she's really motivated in some way. I really don't know why or how. Perhaps it's because I've been giving her special jobs and this is what she needs and probably wants. I kept her jobs to a minimum, however, because there are good children in the class who deserve to have jobs and why should they see that a bad person gets jobs and they don't? What's the sense of being good? This is what I am afraid of and we'll see what happens later.

DISCUSSION

With few exceptions, beginning teachers during their first days and weeks in their classrooms exhibit symptoms of severe emotional and physical stress. This teacher's display of hysteria, weeping, state of near collapse, depression, self-doubt, hostility, and aggression toward some youngsters in her class is not atypical.

Most of us are aware of the tensions and strains accompanying unfamiliar routines or activities. However, the symptoms expressed by beginning teachers, and described so vividly in the preceding incident, go far beyond the ordinary fatigue associated with a new mode of employment. They are surprisingly similar to the phenomenon described by anthropologists as "culture shock."

It is important to remember, however, that the new teacher is not moving into a different culture. She is still in our own society. Nonetheless, the new locale, the unfamiliarity of the people, both staff and children, the sense of containment, the new responsibilities, and the strange routines and problems seem to precipitate a syndrome which has been experienced by many others throughout history when thrust into the unfamiliar life-ways of a foreign culture. Immigrants, tourists, students of other cultures are among those who have experienced this phenomenon.

The symptoms of culture shock have been studied by anthropologists. One of the symptoms is a "ludicrous tendency to raise one's voice to a shout when one finds a foreigner unable to understand simple English." How many new teachers exhibit this same tendency to shout and scold at their youngsters. Other reactions include numbing fatigue, anger against the strangers confronting one, or a frenzied retreat into the familiar. There is often, in addition, a feeling of helplessness and a desire for company of one's own kind.[1]

Why should this happen to individuals who move into

---

[1] Conrad M. Arensberg and Arthur H. Niehoff, *Introducing Social Change: A Manual for Americans Overseas,* Chicago: Aldine Publishing Company, pp. 188–89.

strange situations? The shock and forced readjustment which occur are a result of the strain of heightened attention to strange cues and signs in an unfamiliar environment. The reaction is compounded by frustration, exasperation, and irritation at the strangeness of the situation and the absence of expected responses by others.

Some disturbances always occur for the individual thrust into the strangely upsetting world of the unfamiliar, although the severity of culture shock may vary. Some people are more tolerant of new experiences, and less anxious when faced with new, unusual, and baffling situations. The reasons for this arise from a multitude of factors which include temperament, earlier exposure to similar experiences, greater familiarity with a variety of situations or life-ways, etc. The value of earlier exposure in overcoming or preventing the more acute manifestations of culture shock has been recognized by those who make an effort to employ teachers in schools where they have had experience as student teachers. (It is important to recognize that such prior experience helps overcome the acute symptoms of culture shock—it does not mean the teacher is competent and without need of professional assistance. Her case, generally, does not represent an emergency situation, but culture shock can be experienced more than once.)

For the new teacher, the first few weeks spent in the school are critical, for her attitude toward the children and her occupation can be set positively or negatively during this time. Contempt for the children is one unfortunate possibility. Other reactions may result in serious self-doubt, resulting in the abandonment of teaching completely, or at least leaving the inner-city school where her services are needed.

Most people survive the period of culture shock. They do this by continual exposure to the unfamiliar until it no longer seems strange, unpredictable, and threatening. This requires a concerted effort on the part of the beginner. Retreat into brooding does not help, as this reassuring principal recognized. Survival in this period requires a real effort to get to know the situation. Although problems may continue to exist, it is the initial days and weeks which are the most critical for the beginner.

Given the existence of the phenomenon of culture shock,

how can teachers be helped through this crucial period toward a constructive functioning on their part? It would seem that certain things might help. One, too many new responsibilities ought not to be imposed upon the new teacher too early. Provision for physical relief in the form of time, or preferably a master teacher in the room to engage the children in constructive experiences together with the teacher are of value. To separate the teacher from her class too often may have the negative result of her not gaining enough familiarity with the children.

The pleasant principal who gives offers of general help is not providing an adequate solution. The new teacher herself often does not know what she needs until a crisis develops. This is not a period in which to anticipate creative teaching. Supplies, guides to lessons, and even visiting teachers who take over lessons will help tide the teacher over this early period. Professional conferences, to plan activities jointly, interpret child behavior and learning, to clarify the clerical duties, will help her over this initial period of isolation and desperation, and help her to keep her problem in perspective.

Just as the teacher is experiencing a critical time, so are her pupils. Many of the youngsters, for a variety of reasons including earlier experience, will behave according to the school norms despite the crisis through which their teacher is going. Indeed, as described earlier, beginning teachers report their amazement at the fact that on the first day of school the children knew just what to do. Some children, however, are likely to exhibit the same symptoms she does. Certainly, at this time, the beginner ought not to be expected to cope with the seriously disturbed child. On the other hand, children who are having difficulty adjusting to the new class and teacher, or who are responding overtly to teacher behavior, frightening and confusing to them, are all too often victimized. The danger exists, for them, that they will become the scapegoats in a situation over which they have no control.

Here the principal is faced with a dilemma. His teachers expect his support, and expect him to punish or banish the child they view as the cause of their hysteria. If he recognizes that the teacher's difficulty is only in part a reaction to the individual child, he is faced with the problem of what to do.

Unfortunately, little exists in the school system in the way of non-punitive assistance to tide a youngster such as Bobby over his teacher's initial periods of difficulty. To sit in the office, to have the parent come to hear the child attacked verbally, to be treated as "disturbed" and in need of guidance, to become associated with a "record" that follows him through the school years can early establish the child in the role of troublemaker.

Helping the teacher through his or her initial culture shock must include safeguards against the victimization of children. In this particular case, the principal's sympathy, the support of husband and family and friends, and the removal of the child especially irritating to the teacher helped Mrs. Bender over the critical period of danger. It would be interesting to know what became of Bobby.

Jean acted with hysteria and tears to the school situation just as her teacher had. Unlike her classmate, Bobby—who interestingly enough delivered to the teacher the note Jean had written—Jean made a determined and deliberate effort to investigate for herself what Mrs. Bender's behavior really meant.

Reacting quite differently to Jean than to Bobby, Mrs. Bender demonstrated rather clearly that her punishment of youngsters in the class was not a function of conscious prejudice on her part. Apparently she succeeded so well that Jean, accepting the teacher's explanations, proceeded to have less difficulty in class after that. Together with the problem of prejudice, Jean, after viewing what had happened to Bobby, was unsure as to whether she, as an individual, was being rejected as well. After her discussion with the teacher, this did not seem to be a serious threat any more. Yet the teacher persists in ascribing the value judgments of "good" or "bad" on Jean's behavior, which is not seriously aberrant at that.

Teachers and supervisors working in inner-city schools with large populations must be cognizant of the fact that teacher behavior is viewed in the light of the long and profoundly disturbed history of race relations in this country. Suspicion of the motives of school personnel, accusations of prejudice, etc., are not simply the reflection of agitation which may or may not exist in any given area. Studies of youngsters have demonstrated awareness of race as early as age three. Much of the literature argues that this awareness is associated with a poor self-concept which reflects the dominance of whites in American life over the subordinate role played by Negroes.[2] Recent study has questioned that poor self-concepts are true of all youngsters,[3] and growing pride in race is increasingly characteristic.[4] Undoubtedly, a wide variety of reaction and personal integration of self-concept and attitudes toward whites does exist. Teachers too share the prevailing racial attitudes of the larger society and it is to be expected that they bring prejudice with them.

Mrs. Bender's hysteria and obvious distaste for Bobby provoked Jean into a hysterical reaction as well. But Jean's forthright "laying the cards on the table," so to speak, forced the teacher to considerate, respectful discussion with Jean to clarify the issues. That Jean could now see Mrs. Bender's behavior as not emanating from her own blackness helped improve the climate for learning. The fact that the teacher indicated her respect for the child by inviting her to a discussion to clarify the problem and to communicate better with one another was very valuable, for it is only when effort is expended to understand the meaning of cues in the new environment that the more negative effects of culture shock can be avoided. Whole new fascinating insights that are non-

[2] See, for example, D. Ausubel and Pearl Ausubel, "Ego Development Among Segregated Negro Children," in A. Harry Passow, *Education in Depressed Areas,* New York: Bureau of Publications, Teachers College, Columbia University, 1963, pp. 109–41; Kenneth B. Clark and Mamie P. Clark, "Racial Identification and Preference in Negro Children," in Eleanor E. Macoby et al., *Readings in Social Psychology,* New York: Holt, Rinehart & Winston, 1958, pp. 602–11; and Abram Kardiner and Lionel Ovesey, *The Mark of Oppression: Explorations in the Personality of the American Negro,* Cleveland: The World Publishing Company, 1957.

[3] David W. Johnson, *Changes in Self and Racial Attitudes of Negro Children Derived from Participation in a Freedom School,* New York: Institute of Urban Studies, Teachers College, Columbia University, 1964, p. 35.

[4] David Rogers, *The Lost Generations,* New York, Random House, 1968.

threatening open up to teachers or the students of cultures, who reach the point where they indicate a genuine willingness to listen and learn from one of the young people with whom they would be working.

Mrs. Bender, in describing her week, saw her experience with Bobby as being positive, her experience with Jean as negative. It would seem that the reverse judgment more accurately describes the situation.

CHAPTER 3

Machismo: Culture Conflict in the Classroom

Culture conflict in the classroom can present the danger of rejection and victimization of children when those in charge of their education are unable to understand some of the underlying culture contact and culture conflict problems causing children to engage in certain types of behavior.

Miss Kooper
Grade 6/3

October 12. I really can't explain why Jimmy is particularly more troublesome than the other children. It's just that he calls out all the time. He calls out in Spanish; he talks Spanish. He shows no respect for me. So far, two weeks in a row, I've given a spelling test and he doesn't take it. He just sits there with the paper. He creates a disturbance. He dances in the halls, he dances around, he sings, he calls out. He's always talking! He's always doing something wrong!

On Monday . . . well, Monday is always just a bad day. We have library on Mondays and somehow or other they're quiet while they're in the room. I don't have much of a discipline problem while they're in the room but the minute we go outside someplace it's just bedlam.

We went down to the library and Jimmy was his usual talkative self. He just talked and talked and talked the entire period. I yelled at him. The library teacher yelled at him; she threatened him that he was not going to be able to come to the library any more. It didn't make a bit of difference. He rambled on and on and on in Spanish. He didn't pay any attention to what anybody told him.

Then, later, as we were coming up the stairs he was talking and talking and dancing around. He's the second person in line and the first boy was holding the door, so he was right under my nose. I was standing there waiting for quiet and he was dancing around and running up and down the stairs just making a general nuisance of himself.

I got so mad at him at that moment! I've never really gotten as mad as I did that time. I grabbed him by the tie to make him stand still and he said, "Man, let go! Man, don't do that!"

I just held his tie. I think I probably might have even choked him but he kept on saying, "Go ahead! Choke me, man! I don't care. I don't care."

Finally I said, "When you stand still, I'll let you go."

He wouldn't, just in spite! He just kept pulling away and leaning back. Oh, I was so mad! Finally he just loosened his tie and took it off his head and I was left standing there with his tie in my hand.

This kept going on. As we walked through the halls Jimmy talked and talked. I said to him, "Jimmy, do you remember what Mr. Stark said about putting you back into the fifth grade? Don't think I wouldn't do it!"

He said, "Man, you wouldn't send me to the fifth grade. Nobody sends me to the fifth grade. I don't care."

"Well, we'll see," I said.

He was imitating me now and he said, "I don't care. I'd rather go to the fifth grade anyway. I'd rather have a man teacher; men teachers are more fun. I wish you could put me in the fifth grade."

This continued on and on in front of the whole class and I was really mad.

Finally, Mr. Stark came along. I just looked at him and said, "I don't want this boy in my class!"

He pulled him out of line and asked what he did. I explained what he did and how he was just such a general pest. Mr.

Machismo: Culture Conflict in the Classroom

Stark said he would see what could be done. Ten minutes later, Jimmy's mother came to school. They sent for his father too.

That afternoon, Jimmy tried to get on my line but I said, "Uh uh! You're not in my class. Get off this line!"

"Where shall I go?" he asked.

"I don't care. You're just not staying on this line," I told him.

So he was in the fifth-grade class for about a day. I don't know what happened but the next day Mr. Stark brought him back into my room and said, "Jimmy's here on trial. If he acts up one more time he'll be out permanently."

Of course, Jimmy was very good that day.

On Wednesday, I got a note from his fifth-grade teacher of last year. It seemed that he had started off last year in the same way, as a general nuisance. The note said, "Jimmy is very self-conscious about being short. You have to compliment him and make him feel like a big man in front of the class."

I figured, "All right. I'll try this."

It just so happened that he was good that day and I was really complimenting him, not lying. We were drawing something about Columbus and he draws very well. I held up his picture and praised it and him. For the whole day I just praised Jimmy.

It didn't work! I don't know . . . something happened that he just . . . he went back to his old self. I don't know what's going to happen with Jimmy, for on Thursday I kept ten kids in and he was one of them. He started talking all over again in Spanish . . . jabbering on and on. Once he gets started doing his work he's okay. It's just until he gets down to doing it, and until he stops fooling around long enough to get to work. Once he does begin he's not bad. He's not really too stupid—he's just about at the mean in my class, I guess. But that's Jimmy. If I could make one change in him it would be that he just . . . just . . . maybe if it's really that he's self-conscious because he's short, I would want to make him tall. If I couldn't change that, I would just want him to stop his incessant jabbering in Spanish and making remarks and calling out. He's a pest!

October 19. The most important thing that happened to me this week concerned Jimmy. Last week I told you that he had been taken out of my class and then put back. This week we've been going all out to get Jimmy to be better, to rehabilitate him. It seems to be working very nicely. Before he was very belligerent. Whatever I told him to do was too much for him. He always had a disgusted look on his face. You had to fight with him to get him to do any kind of work.

Now, since Mr. Stark and I have started praising him, and praising him for everything he does, he responds beautifully. I try to overlook a lot of the things that he does—when he calls out, when he says some silly things—I try to ignore him and as soon as he does the slightest little thing properly I'm so glad. "Jimmy knows how to sit. I wish you all could sit as well as he does. . . . Look at this beautiful paper. Everybody's paper should look like this," and all sorts of things like this and he seems to be responding to it.

We had to write some letters. One of the girls in my class was changed to junior high school and I decided to teach them or to review with them the friendly letter. We decided to write to Maria and tell her what had been happening since she left. I listed some points on the board and Jimmy said, "I won't write to her. I don't like her. She's nothing to me and I don't want to write to her."

He was just sitting there and he wasn't doing anything but as I started doing it, he started writing. I was showing them the heading and how to address it and the minute I saw him even start to write I said, "Look at this paper. Jimmy knows how to write a friendly letter. I hope everybody's letter looks like this."

After that he got started and he wrote a beautiful letter. He was fine and everything seems to be coming along well. He still gets a little wild when he wants attention but he's coming along very well.

The other day he brought in a big picture. I don't know where he got it from. It looks like an album cover to a Hercules record. He's very good in art so he was drawing it. I really didn't want him to do this because they were supposed to be doing something else. But he was sitting and drawing and I let him do it anyway. He was so proud when he finished it. He brought it up and I said, "All right, you've finished it. Now I don't want to see it out for the rest of the day."

He asked me if he could paint it. I said he could and he finished it and he put it away and I didn't see it for the rest of the day so I was glad that I had let him finish it. He's a bright boy, and now that I have him participating more he seems to be doing well. His work is improving and his handwriting is improving.

We had a penmanship lesson and Mr. Stark came in while we were doing it. He looked around and complimented everybody on his paper and then he went over to Jimmy and said, "Oh, Miss Kooper, look at this beautiful penmanship. Look at how beautifully Jimmy is writing. Look at that row of G's. Aren't those G's beautiful!" He held up the paper, "Miss Kooper, give me a pencil. I have to check this." He took my red pencil and started checking, "This line of G's is beautiful and look how beautiful this line of G's is." Then he wrote with the red pencil on top "very good," and said, "Jimmy, take this paper home and show it to your mother and show her how nicely you are doing." Then he gave him a special commendation card and put it in an envelope and said, "Now, Jimmy, take this card home and show your mother how nicely you're doing and then bring it back and we'll hang it up with the class's commendations."

I just feel so good that this happened because I really learned something. I was willing once to say, "I don't want him in my class, he's a problem," and be done with it. I would really have been happy with that. Now I see that there is really hope for him and this has taught me quite a lesson—you can help them. I'm so glad now that Mr. Stark kept him in my class because now I feel that he can learn. He's far from being an angel but he does his work now. He stops every now and then but nothing like before. It makes me feel good that something was done after I had all but given up on this boy.

DISCUSSION: THE CASE OF JIMMY

Contact between peoples of different cultures has always presented the possibility of the diffusion of new elements from one society to another. Indeed, the rapid growth of human culture is due in good measure to the ability of societies to borrow from one another and to incorporate the newly acquired elements into their own culture. Those societies with the greatest amount of isolation have developed the most slowly. The highly advanced, complex civilizations of today owe much to their ability to borrow and absorb the cultural experience of others.

In order for cultures to borrow from one another, however, there must be some form of contact between them, either direct or indirect. The nature of the contact can vary from highly sporadic trade contacts to the influence of individual settlers, to complete and close contact between two or more societies.

Complete contacts are exemplified by conquering groups who settled among the conquered. Immigrant groups in America are also examples of continuing and close contact between peoples of varied cultural backgrounds.

Once contact between peoples is made, the processes of borrowing and culture change begin to operate. It is easiest to be aware of the vast debt to culture exchange that our own and other societies owe in the area of technology and material goods. No urban American today, for example, can live through a day without partaking of the contributions of the civilizations of the Orient, the Near East, Africa, aboriginal America, and Europe, via his clothing, housing, and food. The simple borrowing of such traits and goods as cocoa from Africa, tobacco from America, glass from Egypt, cotton from India, etc., has been termed "diffusion" by anthropologists.[1]

However, the process of culture change that takes place when people live in long, continuing contact with one another is more complex than the simple diffusion of traits. Acculturation, the name given to this process, is not a one-sided phenomenon. When two societies are in contact with one another, one does not completely abandon[2] its former culture and completely accept the other. An interchange of ideas and culture elements takes place. This is not an even process, how-

[1] Ralph Linton, *The Study of Man*, New York: D. Appleton-Century Company, 1936, pp. 324–25.
[2] Ibid., p. 335.

ever, and the rate and direction of change are dependent upon many factors.

Several factors enter into the process of acculturation. One is that, in general, contacts between cultures are established through the medium of individuals, and, another, the degree of ease or difficulty of culture change is tied up with the inherent communicability of the culture elements themselves.

While material goods and technological skills move relatively easily between cultures, when one enters the realm of patterns of behavior, attitudes and values, the problem of culture change becomes far more complex. This area lies so often largely beneath the level of individual consciousness, and average members of the society rarely verbalize it even to themselves. Even when there is consciousness and verbalization, it is this area of behavior, values, and attitudes which people tend to consider so "normal," so "natural," as to be unable to comprehend or accord respect to the behavior, values, and attitudes of those different from themselves. This phenomenon, termed ethnocentrism, operates to block communication between cultures. The process of acculturation, therefore, carries with it the possibility of culture conflict which may precede the acceptance or rejection of culture change.[3]

The case of Jimmy is very much concerned with the problem of culture contact, for Jimmy's behavior and difficulty with his teacher can best be understood in terms of conflict between a code of behavior imposed by the school and a code of behavior acted out by Jimmy as a member of Spanish culture.

American elementary school culture is conspicuous for the extent to which children of both sexes are treated alike. By this new teacher particularly, silence, obedience, passivity, self-control, and the use of English are highly valued, for any other kind of behavior is viewed as a threat to her authority, as well as inappropriate in the classroom. These criteria are applied to the boys as well as the girls.

Spanish culture, on the other hand, has two attributes which stand in contrast to the school code. One of these is the definition and acceptance of the "rascal" or engaging

[3] Ibid., pp. 341–46.

rogue personality type, ever in difficulty with authority but always good-humored, using his charm to manipulate his social environment. Jimmy is acting out this culturally accepted role much to the teacher's chagrin. Terribly concerned in maintaining control over the class, the teacher views Jimmy's behavior as threatening to her authority and can think of no more desirable solution than having him disappear. Indeed, she is provoked into rather hysterical behavior by his chattering in Spanish, viewing his talking a foreign language as a threat to herself, and is at first unable to handle the situation in a decorous manner.

Another characteristic of Spanish culture pertinent to an understanding of the problem faced by Jimmy and his teacher is that in Spanish culture male and female roles are very clearly delineated. The "machismo" or cult of maleness presents an ideal role for males consisting of courage, fortitude, the ability to engage in adventurous exploits, and also boasts of sexual conquests as a goal. For women, on the other hand, shame, modesty, resignation, and suffering are considered appropriate characteristics.[4]

Of course, these characteristics of male and female behavior represent the ideal types, and there is in reality considerable variation in actual behavior. Indeed, Spanish women have achieved positions of prominence and achievement in the modern world. Jimmy, however, gives indication of adhering to the ideal Spanish masculine role. He defies his teacher with considerable bravado, considering the many threats she levies against him; he says very clearly that he prefers a male teacher, and he resents having to write to a girl. Her earlier hysterical behavior viewed by herself, as necessary to maintain authority, is so unlike appropriate feminine behavior in Spanish culture that it is not calculated to gain the respect of the child.

The case of Jimmy illustrates the way in which culture conflict can present the danger of rejection and victimization

[4] Julian Pitt-Revers, *The People of the Sierra*, New York: Criterion Press, 1954; Munio Edmunson, *Los Manitos: A Study of Institutional Values*, Tulane University: The Middle-American Research Institute, Publication No. 25, 1957; Elena Padilla, *Up from Puerto Rico*, New York: Columbia University Press, 1958.

of children when those in charge of their education are unable to understand some of the underlying culture contact and culture conflict problems causing children to engage in certain types of behavior. Anthropologists have found that when societies incorporate new elements they do so of their own free will. Forcing a new behavior pattern can make the proscribed elements a symbol of revolt and thus inspire a strong attachment to them. People cannot be forced to accept a new way of thinking or behaving emotionally, although they may act out superficially the required changes. This teacher's use of force caused Jimmy to cling more tenaciously to his behavior and to the use of Spanish. To the child, her resentment and distrust of the use of Spanish indicated contempt for something meaningful to him.

How then are new traits accepted? Principally this occurs on the basis of utility and compatibility. In order to function adequately in the American school environment Jimmy's overt behavior must be modified. On the other hand, the teacher's behavior and understanding as well requires modification.

Fortunately for Jimmy, he is an attractive, bright child with artistic ability. Thus he has personal attributes to which his teacher can relate as well as admire. The child also was fortunate in that his previous year's teacher was perceptive enough to recognize Jimmy's need to feel manly. (This teacher assumed the problem to be one of height, which may have been a projection from American culture that height and manliness go together.) Nonetheless, manliness is a critical factor here and again is very much related to Jimmy's Hispanic background.

Also, in the case of Jimmy, the socialization of the beginning teacher was such that the behavior of the child, which she had initially interpreted as a threat to her authority, was translated for her by another teacher as meaning that Jimmy had certain needs rather than that she was inadequate in the role of teacher. Fortunately, the new teacher was quite happy for Jimmy to feel masculine—thus she wishes fervently that he would grow taller—and she attempted to assume an attitude and to provide experiences which would indicate respect for the child.

She was also helped by the assistant principal, who in very

direct ways participated in indicating to Jimmy that he was well regarded. Not only was the child helped, but also the teacher, by the assistant principal's frequent physical presence and co-operation in regard to the child. His attitude did not indicate to the teacher that she was incapable. He rather co-operated with her in the interpretation of cues in regard to the child, entering the scene in a very positive way. Not the least in importance was the fact that the assistant principal was male. His adult male praise of the child appeared to work miracles. Yet it is precisely male recognition that the boy responds to, for in order for Jimmy to modify his behavior willingly, the new behavior had to be presented as compatible with a masculine role.

The child Jimmy was helped because three very decent human beings were nice to him and began to treat him with respect for his dignity. They made him feel welcome in the classroom by praising his personal talents. Other children not as attractive, bright, or talented might not have received such care, for not every child can behave as an engaging "rascal," manipulating the environment to receive the attention he needs. Cultural understanding on the part of teachers and administrators might help some of them.

The case of Jimmy illustrates a problem of culture conflict in the classroom as it affected one Spanish boy and his teacher. The problem of culture conflict, however, is not confined to the meeting of different ethnic groups in American classrooms. There is another aspect of culture conflict which is highly significant and ought to be considered. This has to do with what anthropologists have termed the discontinuities in cultural conditioning which affect the socialization of children, particularly male children in American society.[5]

The school culture, as was mentioned above, frequently brings with it demands for obedience, passivity, teacher dominance, quiet, order, and provides little differentiation in male and female roles. This is done despite the fact that the larger American culture expects adult males to be more aggressive, more dominant, exert greater independence, and

[5] Ruth Benedict, "Continuities and Discontinuities in Cultural Conditioning," *Psychiatry*, May 1939, pp. 161–67.

Machismo: Culture Conflict in the Classroom

assume more responsibilities than females. In the early school environment, it appears that females are better able to fulfill the requirements for appropriate school behavior. Male children are placed in the position of facing punishment for acting out roles more compatible with their adult status than child status in American society. Also, recent evidence from clinical psychology research indicates wide variation in cognitive style and perception in young male versus female children.[6]

Teachers confronted with large classes and teachers who have little tolerance for individual differences in learning and behavior and little understanding of the cultural implications of behavior, but who regard all deviants as threatening to themselves, are unknowingly, and despite their best efforts, in a position to damage children. The school culture must begin, in order to enable the school to function more effectively as an educational institution, to regard deviance as a cue to improving a learning situation, rather than as an intolerable threat to be met with demotion or placement in "slow" classes.

[6] Professor H. Witkin and his associates of the Downstate Medical Center, State University of New York, have been working on cognitive style and its implications for education.

CHAPTER 4

The Escalator

Misconceptions concerning the nature of cultural experience can lead the teacher to a view of lower-class, minority group children as deficient and limited in their ability to learn.

**Miss Devans
Grade 3/2**

October 5. I went on a trip this week with my children. It was quite enjoyable. We went to the airport. We used the school bus and went with one of the other teachers, the teacher next door and her class. She has thirty-two on her register and I have thirty-one on mine. It was quite an exciting trip.

When we got to the airport I think the thing that impressed my children most was the escalator. None of them or practically none of them had ever seen an escalator before. I explained that it was moving stairs and one girl asked me if it would tickle her feet. Many of the children were frightened to get on the escalator. I think that this experience helped me to understand that these children are from a very deprived background and that in many of the things I have been trying to do with them for the past two weeks I have been assuming that they had the background and intelligence. (I believe that intelligence is closely related to your background because even if you have potential it cannot be developed if you come from a deprived situation.) It helped me to realize that

I was assuming too much about these children. I feel that during the year I'd like to provide many opportunities for these children to gain a wider degree of experience so that they can have a more enriched background, so that they can learn. If a child has never seen an escalator and then reads a story that talks about Johnny going up on the escalator, they have no conception of what that means. I think this is one of the most important things because it did help me to realize the situation that I am in and the situation that the children are in.

DISCUSSION

The term "culture" has been defined by anthropologists in the broad sense, as ". . . that complex whole which includes knowledge, belief, art, morals, law custom, and any other capabilities and habits acquired by man as a member of society." All human beings, if they are to function within the bounds of acceptable behavior and belief as members of their society, learn the culture of their group. Every human society has a distinctive culture[1]—"historically created designs for living, explicit and implicit, rational, irrational, and nonrational which exist at any given time as potential guides for the behavior of men."[2]

Perhaps the most significant contribution made by anthropology has been the demonstration of the very wide variety of distinct, viable cultures developed by man, each shaping its society's conception of appropriate, indeed human behavior. The deep tendency for individuals to be so rooted in their own particular cultural experience, to prefer their way of life above all others, has been called ethnocentrism by anthropologists. Because one's own culture appears so "human," so "natural," it is relatively easy, though not necessary, to move from this ethnocentric preference toward a

[1] E. B. Tylor, *Primitive Culture* (2 vols.), Gloucester, Mass.: Peter Smith, p. 1.
[2] Clyde Kluckhohn and William Kelly, "The Concept of Culture," *Science of Man in the World Crisis*, ed. Ralph Linton, New York: Columbia University Press, 1945, p. 97.

disdainful view of the way of life of others. The history of mankind is filled with the animosities and fears which have existed between the people of distinct cultural groups.

Even the most primitive of human social groups has its culture, i.e., material objects, traditions, ways of living, and a view of the world, related together to form a distinctive ethos. Extremely important too is the fact that in even the most simple, homogeneous society, all members do not have common access to all of the culture. In some societies sex precludes the opportunity of one segment of the population from knowing the skills and lore of the other. In all societies age precludes common access to cultural knowledge.

As cultures become more complex and as more internal specialization develops, the individual is increasingly prevented from acquiring familiarity with all aspects of the culture. In the more complex civilizations, such as our own, the enormous size of the cultural inventory, in terms of material objects, experience, and knowledge of the wide range of acceptable behavior, is obvious. No one individual can ever hope to know all. Each individual has his own unique mastery of particular aspects of the culture, determined in part by age, sex, social class, ethnic group origins, occupation, education, etc. Indeed, the more one learns, the more one becomes aware of all that is yet to be learned.

Yet, as heterogeneous and diversified as is contemporary American culture, all of us have been socialized to be part of it. Americans are regarded as "different" by those of other societies as others appear "different" to us. However, despite the many characteristics held in common, it is the differences among us within the culture which we notice consciously, for these are the things that strike us more dramatically. Those characteristics which mark us as different from the Toda, or Sikkimese, or Hottentot, or Chukchee are ignored, for these are the things which have been internalized and appear so natural as not to count.

The matter of differential exposure to the culture which marks groups within it as "different" is highly significant and ought to be examined in detail, for it will help us understand the confusion experienced by this young teacher concerning her children and the escalator.

The Escalator

Within each subgroup of age, sex, social class, educational level, ethnic region, occupation, there exists a wide variety of differential exposure to the total pool of cultural characteristics of this complex society. So different are the ways of segments of highly complex and large societies such as the United States, that the term "subculture" is sometimes applied to varying sections within it.

Because we assume that the values, attitudes, beliefs, knowledge, skills, and material appurtenances of our own particular section of the culture is *the Culture*, the individual has a great deal of difficulty in understanding that any other area of the culture exists. In addition, there is difficulty in achieving communication with the members of other groups. There are several reasons for these phenomena, so very much akin to the ethnocentrism which exists between cultures. These barriers have been described by Willard Waller:

> *Age is not the only factor that separates people who nominally drink of the same cultural stream from actual community of culture. Mental ability, education, subtle differences of interests and of personality may likewise sort people into cultural pigeonholes. So completely is the individual immersed in the culture of his own age and social level that he often has difficulty in realizing that any other kind of culture exists. He is separated by invisible walls from those about him who follow different gods. Persons living in different segments of our culture, as determined by age and life situation, may find difficulty in communicating with each other or in understanding each other at all. The old cannot understand the young, the prudent cannot understand the heedless, the married can have little sympathy for the unmarried, parents can never commune with non-parents; each person in the world is surrounded by many with whom he must communicate by smoke signals and by only a few with whom he can converse. But the greatest chasm is that which separates young persons and old.*[3]

[3] Willard Waller, *The Sociology of Teaching*, New York: Russell, 1961.

That differences exist between various groups in the population no one would question. The real point at issue in this case, however, is the misconception which exists in the teacher's mind concerning the significance of the children's previous lack of exposure to the culture trait—escalator. To the teacher, knowledge of the escalator, common in her own age and social group, appears so natural that she assumes her children's ignorance of this indicates serious deprivation leading to the inhibition of their intelligence, and, further, precluding their ability to learn. She goes even further and suggests a program of educational intervention in the form of providing more experiences such as the trip to the airport in order that they might then be able to learn.

These are very young children, living in a section of the city without escalators, and previously unexposed to the experience of being on moving stairs. This is not the kind of deprivation of which Piaget and others concerned with learning patterns in children spoke when they wrote of learning dependent on earlier experience. These youngsters were not devoid of sensory experiences, emotions, and interests—they asked questions, talked about sensations such as being tickled, expressed fear and wonder.

This teacher's misconception really is a very common one. It connotes the notion that if you do not share knowledge of "my culture," more, of specific *details* of "my culture," that you are devoid of culture—for the word "deprived" has come to carry with it the belief that the "deprived" lack ability and are crippled by deficits that have prevented them from learning or achieving. This has been carried to such an extreme degree in some instances that children who do not arrive at school fully equipped with the characteristics and knowledge which their teachers have or believe the children ought to have are regarded as "vacuums."

In a study of an American Indian community, Murray and Rosalie Wax described this attitude as it appeared in schools for Indian children, and have termed this phenomenon the "Vacuum Ideology."

By "Vacuum Ideology" we mean the disposition of administrators and school officials to support policies and programs (such as the establishment of nursery schools) with the assertion that the Indian home and the mind of the Indian child are meager, empty or lacking in pattern.[4]

The fact that the children have been previously unexposed to the escalator is no reason for assuming that they cannot learn or develop intelligence. There is the rather obvious fact that human intelligence functioned quite adequately throughout history prior to the installation of the first escalator in 1901. There is also the fact that the children, rather than being "deprived" in the sense of lacking experience, may be quite knowledgeable in other areas, and about other aspects of the culture not shared by their teacher. Also, there is an attitude evident here held by many teachers and administrators that somehow the children ought to come to school already knowing. If children are to learn in school, educators must provide structured learning experiences within the school. If on the contrary, they persist in defining the children as unable to learn because of not coming to school already learned, there is little hope for the youngsters entrapped in a downward-winding spiral of failure.

At a superficial glance, Miss Devans' thinking appears very logical, for she recognizes that, not having been exposed to certain experiences or objects, the children may not understand what they are reading or what the teacher is saying. But the teacher goes further to imply that this means that the children are not capable of learning and that they lack intelligence. Implicit here is a distortion of what has come to be known as the Sapir-Whorfian hypothesis in anthropology and linguistics. Simply stated, this hypothesis maintains that, because the world is presented to us in a "Kaleidoscopic flux of impressions,"[5] it is necessary for these impressions to be ordered. It is through the various patterns of language that

[4] Murray L. Wax, Rosalie H. Wax, et al., "Formal Education in an American Indian Community," Supplement to *Social Problems*, Vol. 2, No. 4, Spring 1964.

[5] B. L. Whorf, quoted in Ralph L. Beal and Harry Hoijer, *An Introduction to Anthropology*, 3rd edition, New York: The Macmillan Company, p. 634.

the ascription of significance to experience is given, and as a result the "real world" is to a large extent unconsciously built up on the language habits of the group. Thus, language and thinking go together, and according to Whorf, through analysis of the grammar of a language one can discern patterns of perceiving experience.

That language is one of the factors influencing perception and the general organization of experience is rarely disputed. However, important as it is, it need not be the only influence, for the social and physical environment of a people play a part as well.

Vocabulary itself is significant in that speakers of one language may by their adoption of the vocabulary of the other indicate their willingness to view the world, i.e., participate, in the way of the other culture. The teacher appears to be unaware, however, that "escalator" is but of limited significance as vocabulary since it is technical jargon, clearly used to describe a mechanical trait of the culture. It is very easily learned since it presents no serious cultural barrier, as might, for example, words describing concepts dealing with appropriate male and female behavior or attitudes toward competition and achievement. The teacher's assumption that the absence of this linguistic trait connotes the absence of intelligence and the ability to learn is unwarranted. The vocabulary of a language clearly reflects the social and physical environment of a people. As the social and physical environment changes, so does the vocabulary, either by internal changes or by additions. Every language has within it the ability to adjust to changed requirements.[6]

The confusion here is a very serious one, for it is not the children's inadequacy which is the problem. It is rather the need for the teacher to concern herself with the problem of communication with a group of youngsters who, in this highly complex society, do not share all of her experiences, just as she does not share all of theirs. Age, social class, occupation, and ethnic origins are all involved as complicating factors.

If the teacher persists in labeling all communication prob-

[6] See Paul Henle, "Language, Thought and Culture," in *Language, Thought and Culture,* Ann Arbor: University of Michigan Press, 1958, pp. 1–24.

The Escalator

lems as indicating deprivation and inability to learn, the children are doomed to failure, for the teacher and the school will then not be looking for those positive aspects of the child's experiences upon which learning can be built. Excursions, trips to fill the "vacuum," to make up for deficiencies, are probably nice adventures for children. In themselves they will not provide for academic success. The use of the mind to imagine, to engage in the spirited adventure of discovery, does not require real experience for everything learned. Men dreamed of moving stairs before their invention. Throughout the world, and throughout history, people told of flying in the heavens ages before the airplane, and many a youngster has reveled in stirring voyages beneath the sea without having been in a submarine. Imagination, vicarious learning, dreams of a better world, journeys to faraway places are all possible via the written word, the spoken story, and the television set. The teacher who is perceptive and concerned with the problem of communications can be a guide to the developing youngster, interpreting for him the strange words, objects, and ideas previously unknown to him.

This well-meaning teacher wishes to provide her charges with many experiences. The danger exists, however, that she will inhibit her teaching for fear that the children will not learn because of their lack of understanding due to deprivation. If she limits their exposure to adventure and exploration of the content of the broader culture to those few times she can arrange actual trips or direct experience, she herself will run the risk of becoming an agent in providing deprivation of experience for the children.

On the other hand, if she concerns herself with problems of instruction, making certain that she and the children understand one another, this need not happen. Children can learn providing their teacher learns to concentrate on the problem of communication and instruction without assigning negative judgments concerning learning ability and intelligence to children who do not, by reason of age and social group, share her particular mastery of a particular section of the culture.

CHAPTER 5

Soap Doesn't Always Clean

This case relates an extreme example of a teacher's punitive handling of the use of obscenity by children in a fourth-grade classroom. It reflects the fact that slum school children often do not give the teacher evidence of fulfilling her role successfully because they do not behave according to her ideal image of what school children should be like. This results in frantic efforts on her part to establish her authority, efforts which prove highly unsuccessful.

**Miss Cedar
Grade 4/2**

October 12. Roger has been arrogant since the beginning of the term and seems to resent authority. If you ask him a question he just looks at you and won't answer. This week, all week, the aides, who are in charge of the children after lunch, have had to discipline him for getting out of line, disrupting the line, and talking. He has been very talkative in class and has not been doing his work: he has had to have his test papers signed because he failed, his homework was incomplete, and his classwork was sloppily and lazily done.

On Wednesday I just got disgusted with his behavior. He had been disrupting the class all morning. He had not had his

Soap Doesn't Always Clean

test papers signed. He had not done his homework and he kept getting out of his seat and raising his hands in front of the other boys.

In the afternoon, after I saw that he had been taken out in the yard again, I had him stand in the back of the room and hold his books. He didn't say anything. He went to the back of the room and smiled. He had a ridiculous grin on his face as if to say, "Make me stand in the back of the room. What do I care? I don't care who you are or what you are." Yet his eyes seemed to be brimming with tears and I wasn't quite sure exactly how he felt.

Well, he was standing in the back of the room with his books and I was trying to conduct a lesson but every few minutes I would hear a crash—Roger had dropped his books. I said, "Pick them up and don't make a sound!"

He dropped them again and laughed. He thought it was very funny—it was good exercise bending down to pick up books.

Finally, after dropping them three or four times, I thought the whole thing was ridiculous. There was no need for him to drop them. I left the lesson and went to the back of the room. I took him by the shoulders and started to reprimand him, "Who do you think you are? This is not funny! There is certainly nothing to laugh at! If you don't know how to behave, it isn't funny. It's a sad situation!"

Then filth came out of Roger's mouth and he was raving mad. "Get the _____ off me!" His arms were swinging, not particularly at me but just to get away from me.

"That's enough from you!" I said, and I took him down to the principal's office.

Mr. James wasn't in his office so I left him sitting in the secretary's outer office. I left a note for Mr. James telling him that Roger had used obscenities in the classroom and asked if he would deal with such behavior. I realized that I couldn't leave this boy in the classroom after doing such a thing. I don't know who heard him or how many had heard him but I know they just knew that something was wrong, and if they had heard what came out of his mouth they would lose all respect for me. So I had to show them that I would not stand for any nonsense and take him down to the highest authority, the principal. This was at about 1:30. At two o'clock, the principal sent up for Roger's clothing and I sent it down. I didn't know what he was going to do.

When I left at three o'clock, I stopped in at Mr. James' office to see what had happened. I first saw the assistant principal, who told me that Roger had been in and out of the office all afternoon like a yo-yo, and Mr. James had spoken to him. When I finally got to speak to Mr. James he told me that he had spoken to Roger and had called his mother and told her that Roger could not go back into the classroom until she came in with him.

When I left, Roger was still sitting on the bench in the outer office so I told him, "Put on your coat and come with me."

He gave me a dirty look and I walked him outside and told him that he was dismissed. All this time he didn't say a thing —he didn't apologize or anything. He just looked at me with a faraway expression on his face.

The following afternoon at about two o'clock Roger finally arrived at my room with his mother and one of the school aides. The aide was necessary as a translator since Roger's mother speaks only Spanish.

The mother wanted to know what had happened and I told her exactly what had happened—about Roger standing in the back of the room, dropping his books, laughing and then using curse words. She said . . . well, this was what I got in translation and, of course, it loses a lot in translation . . . but what she seemed to say was that Roger was a good boy and he never had any trouble in any other school but he didn't like it here.

I told her that whether he liked it or not was no excuse for his using such language. I should have told her off! She didn't even seem angry at the boy. I should have told her "I don't care if you let Roger use this language at home. He's not to use it at school!" I should have made her angry at his behavior.

She seemed to be saying, "He's a good boy. He didn't really do that; you are only imagining it."

Of course I couldn't understand what she was saying and I just got bits of it from the aide, but her attitude was one of, "Oh, my little darling couldn't do such a thing. He's a good

Soap Doesn't Always Clean

boy. I'll punish him but I won't punish him too badly. How could I do such a thing to my little dear?"

"I don't care if he likes it here or not," I said. "If he doesn't like it he doesn't have to stay, but he's never to open his mouth like that again in my classroom!"

Roger was still standing out in the hall, so I said, "Go to your seat and don't say a word!"

He just stood there.

"Get in the room!" I said.

He didn't move. He didn't say a word as usual. Strong, silent act! Finally his mother went over to him. In a condescending way she said (the aide had already left so I could only judge what she was saying by her attitude and facial expression), "Go in the room and be a good boy. Don't do it again." She didn't really reprimand him. "You belong in that room. Listen to the teacher."

I finally piped up and said, "When I speak to you, you do as I say! *I am the teacher here! I am in charge here! Now get in the room!*" [Author's emphasis]

Finally, with tears in his eyes, he came in and took his seat. He was quiet for a few minutes and then, of course, he started chattering again. I said, "If I speak to you once more you're going down to Mr. James' office again."

Well, the rest of the afternoon went quietly after that. I guess the message had sunk in. He didn't like it down in Mr. James' office and he was afraid of going down there again.

At three o'clock, after I had dismissed the class, I went back to Mr. James' office to find out what had happened with the mother. He asked me if Roger had apologized. I had meant to have Roger apologize but I was involved in a lesson and it completely slipped my mind. Mr. James told me that Roger and his mother had promised that Roger would apologize before he was allowed back in the room. This shows the contempt of authority or disregard for authority, disregard for promises, that Roger and his mother have. I told the principal that I would take care of this the first thing in the morning. I would not let him back in the classroom until he apologized.

The next morning when Roger came in, before I let him into the room, I said, "What did Mr. James make you promise **to** do before you came into this room again?"

No answer.

Well I stood out there for a few minutes saying, "What did he make you promise to do?"

No answer.

"All right, if you don't remember you're going down to Mr. James' office again. He can remind you!"

No answer.

"Mr. James told you to say something to me. What did he tell you to say? . . . If you don't say it now you're going down. . . . Mr. James said to apologize . . . so apologize!"

"I apologize," he said.

"That's not enough," I said. *"Say, 'I'm sorry, Miss Cedar. I'll never open my mouth like that again.'"* [author's emphasis]

He finally said it.

"Now," I said, "because you didn't remember to do it when you were supposed to, you can go home and for homework I want a formal letter of apology. I want you to write me a letter apologizing and promising never to do it again."

Well, since then, I haven't had too much trouble. That was all day yesterday and if I did catch him doing the least little thing he shouldn't have been doing—getting out of his seat to sharpen his pencil when he should be in his seat, opening his mouth—I said, "You keep quiet or you go back down to the office!"

The next morning after I came back from Mr. James' office the class was quite good. I think I scared them into realizing that if they didn't toe the line they weren't going to be in this class. If I have trouble with them they are going down to Mr. James' office.

This was important to me because it was the first time such a thing had happened in the classroom, and I could not let it go by. I had to sort of reaffirm my authority and get the point across to the class—the importance of respect for authority. The teacher and other people in such positions cannot be talked to in this way. I think the class has to realize that. Language like this is such a part of their daily lives that I don't think they realize it. Of course, some of them do realize it and they know very well what they are saying when

Soap Doesn't Always Clean

they say it and they do mean to say it. Sometimes, I guess, it just slips out. Roger, I think, knew what he was saying and meant to say it, but he learned never to do such a thing in the classroom again. He says he knows what the consequences are going to be.

I think this whole situation was good in that I now found my class much more co-operative. After this incident occurred they saw that I meant business. If anyone says anything like that again they know they are going down to the office. They are not going to get away with anything and they must respect the authority that I hold over them.

There were more fights in my class this week. When I saw Mr. James he told me to "Talk to the class nicely and tell them the importance of not using our hands to fight. Tell them how we can fight with words and give them a little lesson on it."

So yesterday afternoon before three, I started giving them a little friendly talk. I told them how we were all one big happy family and we should not fight with our hands in school. We have better ways of fighting and I said, "How can we fight?" They didn't know so I told them. "We can tell people something nicely, not in a mean or obnoxious way. We don't have to use our hands and, if we really have a problem, we come and tell the teacher; we don't take it upon ourselves. We're going to be together for the year and we have to get along as one big family. Children who fight don't really belong in our class. This is not the way children in the fourth grade should behave."

They were all quiet and listened very intensively because they realized that it had happened before and they were quite scared about it.

No sooner did I get through with this lesson than I saw this little girl, Rosa, and Tom fighting—for no reason at all. Tom said that Rosa was bothering him but I doubt it because Rosa was sitting on the other side of the room, almost, and Tom started hitting her. I said, "What did I just get through saying?"

"After school I'm going to knock her _____ head off," said Tom, using an obscene word such as the one Roger had used several weeks ago.

"Well," I said, "come to the back of the room, Tom. You and I have some business to take care of."

I wanted to wash his mouth out with soap but he's quite a large boy and I couldn't succeed. He just wouldn't open his mouth enough for me to shove the soap in so I told him, "All right, if you don't want to have your mouth washed out with soap maybe you will go down to speak to Mr. James about it. . . . Apologize to Rosa, especially since we were just discussing this . . . and then you have a fight, with a girl, no less."

He halfheartedly apologized to Rosa without even looking at her, so I said, "All right, down to Mr. James with me at three o'clock." Mr. James, however, wasn't in, so I'm going to take him down on Monday.

I have really reached my limit with this obscene language and swearing in the classroom. This is really quite important and I don't know what I'm going to do to completely alleviate it. I know that it can't go on any longer. It's ridiculous! The other children should not be subjected to it. They must learn that this may be the way they behave in the street but not in the classroom!

DISCUSSION

The case of "Soap Doesn't Always Clean" is an extreme example of a teacher's punitive handling of the use of obscenity by a school child. It appears to be an extreme example because it is difficult to imagine a teacher who passed through a liberal arts education and who herself has been reared in a metropolitan atmosphere literally to equate obscenity with filth and to treat it with soap. Contemporary literature is filled with the kind of obscenity one can hear used by urban school children—"fuck," "shit," "mother-fucker," "screw you," etc. These words have lost a great deal of their shock value due to their overexposure, as it were, despite the fact that they are ordinarily not acceptable in polite company or in schoolrooms. There is a good deal more than the mere use of obscene words which is involved here and it is to these matters that we must turn.

Soap Doesn't Always Clean

Students of social class variations in the teacher-pupil relationship have found that often teachers experience difficulty when confronting children who do not behave according to the teacher's idealized image of what a pupil should be. Referring to this problem, Howard Becker has found that "Often the slum child offends the teacher's moral sensibility because of his family situation, his cleanliness and dress, and his moral behavior. Often the teacher observed that she found the moral behavior incomprehensible. She could not believe that any normal human being would act in such a way."[1]

Clearly, the teacher who is morally offended is likely to display to the children her lack of regard for them, or even her disgust at their behavior. It has already been discussed that this ethnocentric view is not conducive to utilizing the child's experience and values as a means of introducing to him the culture of the larger society.

This case, however, is not so much concerned with morals as would appear superficially, but is rather far more concerned with the difficulties this teacher has in fulfilling her idealized version of the role of teacher. The problems concerning obscenity do not arise until after she has run into other problems with her class.

Miss Cedar's difficulties with Roger stem from the fact that he talked on line in the yard, that he failed his tests, that his homework was incomplete, that his class work was "most sloppy" and "lazily" done, that he was "arrogant" as evidenced by his looking at the teacher but not answering when asked a question, by raising his hand out of turn, and by getting out of his seat.

It is very revealing that the teacher gives no indication of having made efforts to understand why Roger was not doing the things which she considered appropriate and proper for a pupil in her class. On the contrary, rather than consulting with the child concerning his difficulty with homework, rather than interpreting his poor performance and his not answering in class as indicating learning problems to be analyzed and solved, Miss Cedar provides a ready-made interpretation that

[1] Howard S. Becker, "Social Class Variations in the Teacher-Pupil Relationship," *Journal of Educational Sociology*, Vol. 25, 1952, pp. 451–65.

the child is "arrogant." In other words, she interprets his difficulty not in terms of a mutual problem to be solved by the teacher as well as the child, but rather as a deliberate attempt on the part of the child to "get" the teacher, as a threat to her position, and therefore to be treated punitively. Indeed, Roger's behavior *is* threatening to the teacher, for he does not give her a feeling of successful fulfillment of her teaching role. Just as she requires acceptance by the administration, so she needs reassurance from the children that she is functioning successfully. Roger, on the other hand, makes her intensely anxious, for he is evidence that she is not doing very well, and rather than seek the solution by acquainting herself with the meaning of the cues his behavior gives her, she frantically seeks to destroy the cues by punishment and even banishment of the child from the classroom.

Once he has been thus rejected by the teacher, who rather than seeking to help the child and incorporate him into the group sends him to the back of the room to hold books till they drop over and over from his arms, the child lets forth with a stream of obscenity at the teacher. (While this represents an extreme case, it is interesting to note that Miss Cedar learned the "trick" of having the child stand in the back of the room with his arms loaded with books from other teachers in this slum school.) Her punitive handling of the situation continues through her demands for the principal to take firm action against the child, to her terrible distrust of the mother, her lack of respect for the mother's supportiveness, made evident by the assumption that the mother's kindness to the child was also threatening to the teacher's position, although the teacher really didn't understand what the mother said to her son, and through the demands for notes of apology ad infinitum.

The teacher has made it abundantly clear to the youngster that he is unwanted and unwelcome in school. Roger's silence is interpreted by his teacher as insolence and disobedience. Yet silence in the presence of an adult can mean precisely the opposite—a mark of respect given by a Puerto Rican child to an adult. He apparently cannot grovel low enough before this teacher will accept him back in the room, and a genuine feeling of belonging and welcome does not seem to be in the

Soap Doesn't Always Clean

offing. This kind of handling gives a child very little alternative except to express hostility overtly, in the best way this child knew, via obscenity (he does not strike the teacher, although some children might), or hostility in a suppressed manner via apathy, or patterned nonco-operation in the learning process.

This teacher, although morally upset by obscenity, is far more upset by the realization that its use really reflects her lack of authority over the children who are using it. More often than not, children know that obscenity is unacceptable in the school culture, and occasional lapses into its use are not serious offenses if the teacher calmly reminds the youngsters of this fact, or ignores the incident, or discusses the matter in another context.

The use of obscenity can reflect a wide variety of possible significances. For some children, obscene words are such an ordinary part of the linguistic environment that their use is habitual, and sometimes the words themselves almost lose meaning in the repetition. Punitive handling, or moral indignation in such cases is inadequate to achieve a shift in linguistic habit. Examples set by staff and most children in language use are more appropriate ways of teaching an appropriate school vocabulary.

As in this case, however, obscenity also can represent the verbalization of hostility and aggression toward the teacher or toward another child. Here, too, punitive handling and moral indignation are not effective techniques for handling the situation. Miss Cedar's use of corporal punishment, or social isolation, and of derogatory handling of Roger all clearly demonstrate to himself and to the other children in the classroom that she, while not using obscene words, has other, effective techniques for demonstrating *her* hostility and aggression. The children are unimpressed with her pleasant little lecture and proceed to give evidence that she has no control over her class except through the use of terror. Miss Cedar might have had a greater impact upon her charges and demonstrated more adequately her control over the situation if she had been able to maintain her poise initially over Roger's poor class performance, or even later when he did lash out at her verbally. The lesson could have continued, or the class could have been moved to another activity. Roger could have been seen after class, quietly, and in an atmosphere of exploration of the problem. Mistakenly, Miss Cedar views that she had to make an issue in order to gain the children's respect, and as a result she seems to have lost it altogether.

Obscenity can at times be reflective of more serious psychic disturbance than appears to be the situation in the case described here. For help in analyzing this, the teacher needs recourse to professional consultation in the school. Here, too, however, clashes with the child serve little purpose other than to exacerbate the situation.

There is a special form of obscenity practiced among lower-class Negro boys and men known as "Playing the Dozens" or "The Dirty Dozens." Sometimes, among groups of close friends, a verbal exchange of obscene references, generally with regard to incestuous behavior, is engaged in for the pure fun of exercise in the richness and originality of language which can be employed. More often, however, to be "slipped in the dozens," i.e., to be the recipient of one of these verbal taunts is to be so challenged that one is required to respond either by further verbal retorts or by violence. Failure to respond is to cast aspersions upon one's masculinity and to suffer severe loss of face in the eyes of one's peers. This view is so widespread that even Negro men who have risen to the middle class and no longer accept the folkways associated with "Playing the Dozens" require self-control when the dozens are "slipped" to them.

This subcultural pattern is widespread among lower-class Negro men. Thus the use of obscenity and the outbreak of violence associated with it which sometimes occurs among Negro boys in slum schools are often associated with "Playing the Dozens." The use of obscenity by Negro male lower-class children is a fairly deliberate, meaningful thing. Obviously, such behavior runs contrary to the school culture, and in addition is often offensive and strange to the teacher. Thus, the child who lashes out against another child may appear to initiate a fight and is often punished, when he is doing the only appropriate thing he can to defend his masculine iden-

Soap Doesn't Always Clean

tification in the eyes of his peers, and in terms of his own self-respect.

This is not to argue that teachers ought to condone or accept "Playing the Dozens." However, if the teacher is cognizant of the behavior pattern, and she witnesses behavior between boys which appears threatening, a comment such as "This isn't the place" can serve to provide a respectable means for ending the violence or verbal abuse without loss of face for the participants. It may establish the teacher as "down," or "hep," or "clued in," or any of the other terms connoting knowledgeability. Shouting, punishing, banishing from the class, or contempt for the child who excuses a fight by saying "He called me a name" will accomplish little, for the need to respond to being "slipped in the Dozens," whether or not the children actually know the name of the game, is an integral part of establishing male identity for the child who subscribes to this subcultural pattern.

While sometimes Negro girls do play the Dozens, it is generally regarded as inappropriate and awkward, much the way a girl playing fullback in a football game might be. Should a boy challenge a girl, she, if behaving appropriately, would refuse to engage in the exchange. For very much the same reasons, teachers are not regarded as appropriate participants in the Dozens game; this is a matter which is the province of male peers. Occasionally, some teachers attempt to establish rapport with lower-class Negro boys or try to maintain discipline by "speaking their language," i.e., by using some obscenity. This is a questionable technique not only in terms of its lack of respectability in the school milieu, but also because of the possibility that it might be interpreted as an attempt to engage boys in the Dozens, a threatening rather than a rapport-establishing situation. Such tactics are not only unlikely to establish rapport but also run the risk of strengthening contempt for the teacher who ought not, in the view of the boys, to be behaving in this way.[2]

In an attempt to maintain her stance as an authoritarian teacher, Miss Cedar has resorted to assistance from the prin-

---

[2] For a discussion of pupils' reaction to the use of obscenity by a teacher, see Estelle Fuchs, *Pickets at the Gates,* New York: Free Press (Macmillan), 1967, Ch. 7 and 8.

cipal and the parent. Interestingly, she has not previously called upon the parent to aid in the diagnosis of Roger's learning difficulties. And now, she wishes the parent to support her in the suppression of behavior. Parents have really limited control in such situations. They can urge their children to be "good," but they have no control over teacher behavior which taunts and provokes a youngster into doing the things he does. They can train their youngsters to remain controlled in the face of such provocations, but this is at no small emotional expense to the child, and often the parent appears to have no control over him.

In the same way, the teacher has called upon the principal to assist her in maintaining her position. Now, this places the principal in a rather difficult position. Obviously, this principal is not as anxious about obscenity or jousting as is the teacher. He attempts to assure her that these are sometimes typical of the child's milieu outside of school and really not terribly serious. He urges her to instruct the children in modes of behavior appropriate to the school and the public world for which the school is preparing the youngsters, i.e., talk, discuss, and argue, do not fight.

At the same time, however, the principal is in the position of having to back up his teachers. If he does not support them in the actions they take, as for example in the case of Roger, he runs the risk of his staff regarding him as untrustworthy and of letting them down, and of not respecting their professional integrity. Thus the principal calls in the parent, requires that Roger apologize, and even checks to see that the teacher is satisfied with the actions that have been taken. He is reflecting an ambivalent position, for he attempts to return the child to the class in as graceful a manner as he can, yet he must operate as if the child were the only problem, rather than that the child's behavior in part reflects the teacher's handling of the situation. He seems to be aware that he ought to train the teacher in how to approach such problems as obscenity and fighting in the classroom, yet his behavior operates to place the child in the position of victim, because of the need to stand behind his teachers. Also, the slum school principal is invariably caught up in the myriad pressures and demands of his position, and his handling of

Soap Doesn't Always Clean

situations like the one posed by Miss Cedar and Roger appears in the nature of routine smoothing over of crisis situations. The more serious matters of Miss Cedar's difficulty as a teacher and her inability either to provide constructive learning experiences for her charges or to diagnose the causes of learning disabilities in some represents the more critical problem, and the one ideally to which the supervisors of teachers ought to be attending.

The use of obscenity, then, can best be understood if examined within the cultural situation in which it takes place. Whether or not it represents habitual speech and aids in the communication between peers sharing a common tradition, whether or not it represents hostility and aggression, or whether or not it represents severe psychic disturbance can be understood only upon examination of the particular incidents of use.

Exaggerated responses to the use of obscenity by children as evidenced by some teachers is reflective of a variety of causes—moral indignation which comes from ethnocentric views of lower-class culture; fear of the loss of control and authority is another. There are of course psychological components to the flexibility or rigidity of teachers as they respond to children who appear to threaten them, but most important is the threat which comes as a result of children behaving in ways which do not coincide with the teacher's conception of how children ought to act. When the behavior of the children is widely disparate, and for some teachers this means the inability to give the teacher evidence that she is successfully teaching, and the use of language is such as she considers totally inappropriate in the school, her own security in the status of teacher is highly threatened. Miss Cedar chose to confront her children by acting out what she believed to be appropriate evidence of her position of authority over them. The children have responded by continued "misbehavior," for she has chosen to give further evidence to them that she is really not teaching, and they continue to give her evidence that they know it.

CHAPTER 6

The Dumping Ground

It would be misleading and inaccurate to interpret all behavioral difficulties as teacher- or school-induced. The following cases illustrate the confrontation of teachers with children exhibiting symptoms of physical and mental pathology. Sometimes the beginning teacher's classroom becomes the "dumping ground" for those children other teachers are unwilling or unable to handle.

Miss Seabold
Grade 1/5

October 12. The most important thing that happened to me in my school this week was the arrival of Lawrence Brown. Lawrence has been a truant since the beginning of school. He had previously been in kindergarten last year in the same school. On his record it was indicated that he was physically and mentally disturbed.

On Thursday morning the guidance counselor from the school asked to speak with me. She informed me that Lawrence would be in my class today—that was Thursday. She told me briefly about his case. Lawrence is suffering from an aphasic speech difficulty. He is eligible for a special class in a special school. His parents did not wish Lawrence to attend school this year unless he would be given special help. He has

The Dumping Ground

been attending the Eye and Ear Hospital, and has been getting help there.

He is eligible for this special class and his parents have been telling him that he will be going to a new school on a bus this year. As of now, there is no room in this special class for him, and the authorities insist that Lawrence must attend school. Thus, since he is on my register, he must be in my class. The counselor told me that from her speaking with him for the first time, he seems to be a well-behaved child. Occasionally he is able to utter words. She told me of an instance of his calling his little brother to come back, and his words were enunciated correctly.

Lawrence is of Puerto Rican background. The counselor told me both parents seem very, very interested in helping the child. At twelve o'clock on Thursday, Lawrence entered my class for the first time. The counselor also told me that the principal has suggested that Lawrence be seated near my desk, be given special attention, and I must keep an anecdotal record on his progress. Lawrence came on line Thursday. I put him next to a child who speaks good English and Spanish. When we got up to the classroom, many things happened with Lawrence.

I had him seated near my desk. He followed directions very well, and he seems to be a well-behaved child. He was sitting there quietly with his notebook and his pencil and his cookies. As I got into the routines of the day, etc., things were going along just fine, when all of a sudden I heard a terrible sobbing from Lawrence. I went over to him and his hands were shaking. I began to pat him and reassure him that everything was going to be fine, but his sobbing continued. The whole class began to laugh and stare at him. I quickly told them to stop and to go on with their work. The class was then quiet. I continued to try to reassure Lawrence but to no avail. I asked him if he wanted to do several things, such as color, or maybe read a book by himself, but to this he answered "No" by shaking his head. I finally got him out of his seat, and I told him to come into the hall with me; meanwhile, I had one of my monitors stand in front of the class, and I told them to be very quiet.

In the hall, I continued to try to reassure Lawrence—ask

him questions, and pat him—but nothing seemed to help; he continued sobbing.

Finally, Miss Frank, the teacher trainer, appeared in the hall. She asked if she could help me, and I said "Yes." She came over and I briefly told her of Lawrence's condition, and that it was his first day in school this year. She tried, and nothing worked either. She told me to put Lawrence back into the classroom, and if his crying continued and became unbearable, I should call for help. Meanwhile, she came into the class and watched me do a lesson in word study with the children.

Lawrence continued crying for about an hour. I occasionally went over to him and said something reassuring. Finally, he stopped crying, and he was fine for the rest of the day. When we went down to recess, Lawrence's hand was up to participate in the games, and I let him do so. While we were singing some of the songs that go with the dances, Lawrence's mouth was moving, but it was very hard for me to detect whether he was actually saying the words or whether he was just mouthing them. When we got up to the classroom a little later on, I asked him if he was able to say my name. He shook his head yes, and I started to prod him on by saying, "Miss, Miss," and finally Lawrence came up with my name, and I was very, very happy and I told him, "Very, very good." As I said, Thursday was fine, after that.

On Friday, Lawrence came on line with the other children, and I noticed immediately that his hands began to shake. He was whimpering a bit and he kept looking back at his mother, who was standing out in the vestibule with the other parents. I took Lawrence off the line and had him walk in with me. I kept reassuring him, and by the time we got up to our classroom, his whimpering had subsided. The day seemed to be going uneventfully—that is, with Lawrence. He was doing writing with the class, and he had his book turned to the page that we were reading from. He seemed more at ease than he did the day before until about 3:30, when we began to get ready to go home. At a quarter to four, the children were beginning to line up, and all of a sudden Lawrence yelled out, excuse the expression, "pee-pee." I quickly had Lawrence go to the bathroom with another boy in the class. But it was too late, the puddle was already left. He didn't say anything else to me, and, since we were going home, there was nothing that I could do.

I had felt quite apprehensive about Lawrence coming into my class and was very uneasy. After all, he is definitely a problem, whether it's behavior or whatever. The child does not belong in a normal class. It is hard for me to say even what might occur. The guidance counselor said that she's sure that he will be taken out of the class. Also, once a week he may get special help from one of the speech teachers in the school, if she has time to put him on her program.

As of now I don't feel that uneasy for myself, but I do feel uneasy for Lawrence. I really can't empathize with him but it is very easy to notice the strain and tension that he is under. I do hope that he will get helped, but whether it is in my class or whether it is in the special school, I don't know. Many of the teachers have said that he'll probably be in my class for the rest of the year, but I do hope that there is an opening for him in the special class so that he can be helped.

**Mrs. Bender
Grade 5/2**

December 14. I was having trouble with Anita and Freddy, both of whom are discipline problems and who had been referred to guidance. I sent a note down to Mrs. Rogers, the guidance counselor, telling her about Freddy and about Anita. No, I had sent the note to Dr. Frost, the principal, for he had told us that he didn't want us sending children into other classrooms if they were poor in discipline and we were not to send them down to the office or to the guidance counselor. We are first to send a note. So I sent a note to Dr. Frost. He, in turn, sent the note to Mrs. Rogers. All this is time-consuming. Mrs. Rogers got the note, read the note, wrote me a note saying that her office is full. She will call for them later.

In the meantime, upstairs in my room, all hell was breaking loose as far as Freddy was concerned. Anita had calmed down already and what was I to do? Stand there and wait for the counselor to call for him?

I was wild. I spoke to the UFT chairman and I spoke to a

few teachers in the school and I said, "What are we to do? We can't send them to other rooms. We can't really do anything with them." So Mrs. Rogers came up to me after lunch and she said to me, "You know, Janet, you really shouldn't send a child down to guidance if the child is bad. You are defeating the purpose." So from this I assumed that she meant that we are only to send down a child when he is good, but if a child is good, why send him out of the room to the guidance counselor? This is just something I could not understand and a thing that upsets me and bothers me tremendously.

As far as the principal goes, he has no idea what's going on in the classroom. He came from a good school and he just doesn't realize that when he speaks to these children he speaks on an adult level. These children can hardly understand English, so how can they understand what he is saying? He also makes it pretty hard for the teacher to be able to get rid of a child from her classroom. Now, this Anita is a girl who was transferred this week from 5/4 to my room officially. Before that she had been sitting in for two weeks. She was a discipline problem and a behavior problem in her other class and Dr. Frost had sent Mrs. Rogers up to speak to me to find out if I could take her and I said, "I'll try. I'm not saying yes and I'm not saying no. I'll try it."

So I've been trying it and she was good up until the time I got my notice that she was being transferred into my classroom officially, and now when I'm having trouble they are not giving me a way out. I do them a favor by taking the child and now she is upsetting my class. At times she is basically a good girl. But she upsets my class and now I don't have a way to turn. I don't have a way out. It's as if a vise is closing in on me and I keep getting more and more discipline problems in my room. My good students don't get the opportunity to learn.

We are not given the opportunity to discuss things with the principal because he speaks out of both sides of his mouth at the same time and things are just piling up so that I just don't know where to turn any more. The principal does not reward the children. That's certain. Once he does get a child down in the office for discipline, he yells and hollers and he screams and he rants and he raves, but he doesn't reward

The Dumping Ground

them! The only type of reward he does give is by sending them down to the guidance counselor. The children enjoy going there and perhaps this is what Mrs. Rogers had meant when she said "you are only defeating the purpose," but I was under the impression that my purpose was to teach. I'm not a policeman.

Thursday was the day when I almost handed in my resignation. I just felt that there was no place for me to turn.

Dr. Frost had come into my room after Freddy and Thomas had had a fierce fight in the classroom, and he asked me about Freddy's record. Now, Freddy had just been transferred into my class; he was just admitted three weeks ago. I received his records only last week and I have not had the time to go through them. I told him, also, that I didn't like to make a practice of reading records before I knew the child. He told me that I was supposed to read them and I said that I disagreed. Then he said something to me which really made me feel very, very bad. He said, "When you have had twenty years' experience, then, perhaps, you can disagree with me."

This was the first time I had ever said I disagreed with him. I always went along with what he said because he was the principal and he had feelings and he had experience where I didn't. I felt that he was very wrong talking to me like this and I was very upset. New teachers sometimes see things that are hackneyed or that are in bad need of change and . . . oh, this wasn't a case that he had any right to . . . true . . . I should read the records but I feel that the opportunity will arise where I will read them. Until such time I feel that I really don't want to know, because every child is an individual and he's just justified on his own. I don't want to have in the back of my mind comments made by other teachers. Dr. Frost said to me, "Well, that's the purpose of the record card. You should know what the other teachers thought about him so that you will know how to handle him."

I really feel that by reading a record card you cannot understand how a child reacts. I have a case in point right in my class. A boy, Carlos Pizarro, who was in 5/3, who was transferred to my class because of discipline problems in that class. Carlos is reading at lower than second-grade level and

I haven't read his records. I've just been told by word of mouth that he was a discipline problem in his class and that's why he was changed, but I have no problem with him. He's a good child in my room. He's quiet. He's co-operative. He's a marvelous artist and if I had read the record on him before, I'd probably have a negative attitude toward him and wouldn't have expected things from him. I don't know anything about him except that he was transferred from 5/3 and he is behaving beautifully.

I really feel that Dr. Frost was wrong in telling me what he did. It was sort of a slap in the face and I think I've done plenty of things for him. He had no right to say that to me. I've already taken three discipline cases from other classes and I have been offered no outlet at all for these problems. I think it was very unfair of him. I had done everything that he told me to do even though I thought he was wrong. I mean, after all, I am a new teacher. I have no experience, so who am I to say anything. You haven't been told to read the record card or not to read the record card and he tells you that. I mean, that is really something that I feel that he was very wrong in and I don't think I can ever forgive him for that.

January 4. The most important thing that happened in the school this week entailed the small class that I had on Thursday. Thursday was the first day back after the Christmas vacation and fourteen children were absent and I was really amazed at how much we were really able to accomplish insofar as not having so many discipline problems—perhaps it was because the discipline problems were absent, but nevertheless it was a small class. Anita was absent but Freddy was there and other difficult children were there. I was able to give them much more individual attention and work with them. I felt at that time that it was the most wonderful thing that ever happened to a teacher in this type of a school—to have a small class. A class of thirty-four is just too cumbersome— just an impossibility at times—but if the class is small I feel you can really accomplish, really work with these children and give them the TLC—tender, loving care—which most of them really, really need.

January 11. Freddy was one child who gave me the most difficult, trying moments or hours or days this week. The most outstanding things I am embarrassed even to talk about. It was Wednesday, during reading lesson. The class was quiet and this obviously bothered Freddy. He was upset by something that had happened, I guess, at home that day. I don't really know. He was just terrible that day. And then finally he was quiet. All of a sudden while I was talking to the class Freddy interrupted and shouted out, "Mrs. Bender, what color are your panties?"

I was just so shocked at the whole thing I just didn't know what to say. I knew that I had to ignore him and make believe that I didn't hear him. That is what I did. Of course, the rest of the class were all embarrassed for him. And perhaps they were shocked, because first they were quiet and what he did didn't seem to dawn on them right away. Then suddenly they started to laugh and I assume that they were laughing at him. It was just a pathetic thing.

Also, on Thursday Freddy came into the room with his fly open. To help him avoid any embarrassment, I whispered to him that his fly was open. So he said to me, "That's not a fly. It's an airplane. Want to see what's inside?"

I feel this child is definitely disturbed. I thought so before but this certainly puts the clincher on it.

That same day Dr. Frost came to my room and was quite upset with the events that had been happening during the week. He asked me how things were going and I just told him. Then he saw Freddy walking around the room while the rest of the children were seated and busy working and he wanted to know why Freddy was out of his seat. I was very sarcastic at this point because I didn't care any more. I said, "I'm trying to understand. I've been told by guidance people that you have to understand these children, and as far as understanding is concerned, I feel the less I speak to him the better off I am going to be."

"Why?" he said. "What happened?"

Then I told him the incident that had occurred in the classroom that had embarrassed me no end. I told him I had informed the counselor about it and she had said to me,

"Janet, you really must try to understand these children. They don't mean it personally."

When I told Dr. Frost what Freddy had said, he just froze in his spot . . . where he was standing, and said, "Oh, my God!"

He took Freddy out of the room for the afternoon and it was just marvelous. I had no problems whatsoever. We worked very hard and we got much accomplished. This is the first time in a long time that I feel that we really learned and accomplished something. As far as Dr. Frost understanding and taking Freddy out of the room is concerned, I was very, very elated. Finally I understand that I am getting help from the principal and I feel that perhaps this might be more advantageous to me because before I had no outlet for these problems. I used to take them home with me and it was just reaching the point where the job was affecting my health and my home life. I feel finally he has understood my problem. He has read the anecdotal record on Freddy and he has forbidden the boy to go to gym. He said that every time the class goes to gym Freddy will report to his office, and as far as I'm concerned, I couldn't be happier.

Dr. Frost also told me . . . he said that whenever I feel upset . . . and he obviously could see how upset I was . . . when I was upset and things bothered me I should come to him and discuss it with him rather than take it home and be upset by it. So I intend to do just that. Of course, I won't do it for just little things that come up in the classroom. He has his own problems and does not have to be worried about mine.

DISCUSSION

The failure of teachers to establish authority on the basis of internal group structure, the problems of culture conflict, class conflict, and value differences help explain many school-induced problems for children. However, in any compulsory educational system dealing with vast numbers of people, there are bound to be problems of a physical or psychic order over which the teacher has little or no control. Just as it would be

The Dumping Ground

highly improper to diagnose all behavioral problems in school as emanating from mental or physical pathology, so would it be equally misleading to interpret all behavioral difficulties as teacher or school-induced.

School systems recognize the existence of children physically and/or mentally disturbed. Special education classes are provided for children who cannot function in the ordinary classroom, and there are screening procedures to segregate youngsters from the normal school environment who are unable to function within it. Several problems exist in connection with this. Among them is the danger that those removed will be unable to acquire the education necessary for them to move into the larger society; that the milieu in which they are placed is not necessarily therapeutic, but rather punitive; and that children not screened carefully enough may be removed from the normal school environment unnecessarily.

The most serious problem of all, however, is that so often the special environment required best to treat the abnormal youngster is not available to him because of the dearth of facilities and trained personnel. For this reason, it is not unusual for teachers to have in their classrooms children who require special, therapeutic assistance if they are to develop into healthy people.

These two cases illustrate what can happen to teachers when confronted with such problems. One case concerns itself with a child who suffers from a speech handicap—the cause of which is difficult to determine. The other concerns a child whose acting-out behavior is intensely disturbing to the class as well as the teacher and whose behavior may be evidence of a serious psychic problem.

Each case has been handled rather differently by the administration of the school. In the case of the boy with the aphasic speech difficulty, the teacher was briefed by the counselor concerning the boy's case history. In addition, the principal had concerned himself about the case and advised a course of action. His one suggestion that the teacher seat him near herself indicated his sympathy and concern for the child. This was helpful to the teacher in that it was a recommended course of action she could take. The other suggestion was to keep an anecdotal record. Since the school was required to take the child, the anecdotal record, if very negative, could then be used to show higher authorities in order to have the child removed. The significant thing here is that the teacher had been taken into the confidence of the counselor and principal, was informed of the child's difficulty, and could see him as troubled, rather than as a threat to herself and her class. Also, because the child's illness appeared in the form of a physical disability, aphasia, it was treated with compassion.

On the other hand, it is extremely difficult to treat disruptive behavior with compassion. In our own culture it has only been within recent times that even the severely mentally ill have been treated sympathetically and with concern for their lack of ability to function acceptably. Historically, the mentally ill have been treated in Western culture as evil creatures to be tormented, subjected to punishment and banishment.

Schools reflect the growing tendency in society to regard aberrant behavior as a reflection of mental illness or personality disorder. Children who are behavioral problems are viewed increasingly as being in need of professional assistance to enable them to accommodate themselves to the requirements of functioning within the institution. The expansion of guidance services is a reflection of this trend.

It is, of course, true that labeling disruptive children in school this way and placing the burden of adjustment on them often ignores the essential health of those who are reacting to institutional constraints that may in themselves be seriously in need of correction. Thus, while providing more compassionate, supportive services to children, placing the burden of adjustment upon the children may draw attention away from the inherent faults of the institution that require modification. At the same time, the facilities of the guidance services are sometimes the one place where children experiencing difficulties with teachers in school receive adult support, for although it has become increasingly fashionable in schools to label disruptive children as mentally ill or disturbed, it is still easier and more common for the teachers who confront the children in the classroom to view them as "bad" or "evil" children, to be treated in a punitive manner or with banishment. Thus, the disruptive child is conveniently removed from their classes by teachers who complain more vociferously and from a position of greater power, and for the child to be transferred into some other class when the guidance office or the principal's office is too full to detain him.

Our second teacher is new in the school and has been accepting children who have been removed from other classes because of discipline problems. It is distressing to her that her class has become a sort of dumping ground, and when she begins having difficulty with the children, she finds little place to turn. She receives the children with no briefing concerning their case histories, and even if she were capable of adequately analyzing their records, they often arrive long after the child, incomplete and not very meaningful. Comments about the child written on records follow them through school. The teacher correctly recognizes the danger inherent in being influenced by prejudicial, negative judgments made about youngsters by others. When she finally does confront the principal concerning a particularly disturbing child, it is interesting that he condemns her for not studying the records, instead of asking her for a review of the child's behavior in her class, and he does not offer to examine problems in a more professional manner by calling together the teacher, the guidance counselor, and others for discussion.

The teacher, finding no channel of communication open to her concerning her problem with a highly disruptive youngster, becomes bitter, estranged, and almost ready to quit. The principal becomes involved and takes action only after a crisis has arisen, a crisis for which the teacher and the school have been unprepared by virtue of not examining more carefully the child's behavior, already known to be disruptive. The pattern of neglect has nearly destroyed a new teacher and her class, and it certainly has not helped the child.

The principal takes action, interestingly enough, only after the child has exhibited behavior with sexual overtones. From the teacher's report it is, of course, difficult to determine how serious this symptom really is. The guidance counselor, when she hears of the reference to panties and male genitalia, tosses it off as not serious, and urges the teacher not to take it personally. Perhaps this is indicative of culturally induced behavior in a child accustomed to a great deal of open sex talk around him. On the other hand, these references may very well be symptomatic of deeper psychic disturbance. In any event, the precocious heterosexuality evidenced by his references are highly inappropriate. The school culture in general suppresses overt heterosexual overtures. For a child to approach her in this way, and within hearing of the other children, is shocking and embarrassing for the teacher. It also proves distressing enough to the principal for him to remove the child, temporarily, from the classroom, and prevent him from going to gymnasium where there is opportunity for greater physical contact between the children.

Despite the differences in administrative handling of these two cases, and despite the difference in feeling toward the children displayed by the two teachers, the effects upon both classrooms are similar. In both cases, the energies, attention, time of the teacher have been absorbed by the aberrant child to the neglect of the other pupils in the classroom. There has been interference with learning. The class sizes are such that the teacher, faced with the demands of the abnormal child, is unable to work as effectively as she might with the others. If there were smaller registers this might not be so serious a problem.

Certainly greatly expanded services to deal with physical and emotional problems are required. Since these are unlikely to spring into being immediately and be fully capable of handling all problems in schools, it behooves administrators to take care that the beginning teacher's classroom does not become the dumping ground for those children others are unable or unwilling to handle. In addition, unless the teacher is consulted and made to participate in decisions and actions concerning the children, her development as a committed teacher is likely to suffer, for she too is victimized by the situation. Not every problem can be understood in terms of teacher inadequacy. Some children are truly ill and require far more assistance than the teacher is able or can be expected to give.

CHAPTER 7

Fatigue: The Lesson Plan

> Approval by those in authority in relation to her confirms the teacher's view that she is performing satisfactorily in her position. Administrative delay in defining expected performance and delay in helping the teacher achieve satisfactory performance compound the tensions and fatigue of the early weeks.
>
> Mrs. Bender
> Grade 5/2

October 12. The most important thing that happened to me this week in school really happened to me yesterday. That was when my teacher trainer, Mrs. Roman, had a meeting with me concerning plan books.

Previous to my appointment here as a teacher I had had no background in planning. I walked into the school situation not knowing how to write a plan. I had written only one plan during my four years at college, and only one unit plan, which was never collected or looked at. I really was up a dark alley and didn't know what to do. Up until this week I have been writing plans that were collected. Mrs. Roman and the principal went through the plan books of all the new teachers together.

I had received my plan book back with a note saying that I should put an aim into the reading lesson, and some other things. The most important thing, as far as Mrs. Roman was concerned, was that I write an aim for each of the headings I had in the plan book.

Well, I did as she said, and at yesterday's meeting she went over the plans that I had made for this week. She said she was very happy that I had included the aim that I was supposed to. She even said that I should be certain to keep my plan as a model for her teachers next year.

I really was amazed because at first I hadn't known how to start a plan—where to start the first time I did write one. It took me, I think, about five hours on Sunday, the first week of school. I was just going out of my mind. I didn't know what to do and I called up some of my friends. They are also new teachers and they gave me some ideas. After that it took me about three hours to write plans. The funny thing is that last week, it took me only two hours to write the plans, and these are the ones she liked so much.

DISCUSSION

Teachers, like the children in their classrooms, come with a wide range of preparation for the tasks they are expected to perform within the school environment. Part of the teacher's function is to prepare her work, and because she is not in full professional status she is subject to inspection concerning her plans.

The education of teachers is so highly variable that supervisors cannot assume that teachers are prepared in all the areas that might be expected. Changes in the teacher-education institution may appear to be an obvious need. But this remains only a partial answer, for the teacher, no matter how carefully educated, must still learn the specific expectations and requirements of the particular school in which he or she is working.

In this school there is great concern on the part of the supervisory staff and the principal that each lesson plan follow a specific format. Now, it must be pointed out that the plans in the book and the actual behavior of teachers and children, as well as events within the classroom, are fre-

Fatigue: The Lesson Plan

quently very different things. The teacher soon learns, however, that she can win approval if she learns to write out the plans according to administrative requirements. There is nothing automatic about superior or improved teaching following from this. Of course, thinking through the kinds of things the teacher would like to accomplish is worth while. But the emphasis upon form in this kind of plan and the type of conference reported by the teacher give evidence of the neglect concerning many areas which represent problems to the teacher, primarily the area of establishing a working relationship with the children.

There is here too evidence of unnecessarily compounding the physical and emotional difficulty associated with the beginning of teaching. A great deal is heard about the teacher's need to be creative and to be the master of her classroom. But beginners find the whole phenomenon of teaching overwhelming, and certain difficulties faced by a beginning teacher could be avoided. For example, in this school there is a professional assistant assigned to help the beginning teachers. Yet for three weeks this teacher has been preparing what her supervisors consider to be inappropriate plans, spending unnecessarily long and emotionally grueling hours over them, and being in a position that enables her to consult only with other inexperienced colleagues to learn what she might do. To have to "find herself" in this way seems to be unnecessarily wasteful of her energies, and also subject to the danger, from the administration's point of view, of getting poor advice from others not necessarily more knowledgeable than herself.

A more logical approach would appear to be not to allow failure and distress in relation to lesson planning to develop in the first place. This does not mean that the beginner must be told what to do via commands or directives. Rather, time, facilities, and the services of the professional adviser would seem to be best directed initially to joint planning and evaluation of actual classroom situations, so that the planning is related to the real class needs. Possibly at the beginning the presentation of suggested plans, subject to modification by the teacher to suit herself and her children, would be of value also.

Not only would these steps help to relieve the teacher of the anxieties accompanying her insecurity—and help to prevent unnecessary physical fatigue—they might also serve to ensure that the children do not face a month of schooling with a teacher who is not very clear about what she is doing.

PART III

HELP!

CHAPTER 8

The Rexograph Machine

Teachers start their careers expecting further professional development and colleague relationships with their supervisors. It comes as a rude shock to them to find that they are treated as low-level bureaucratic functionaries. This case illustrates the conflict that arises between professional and administrative authority within schools and the effect of the conflict on the teachers.

Miss Harris
Grade 2/6

October 12. The teachers of classes 2/5, 6, 7, 8 were called in for a special conference with Miss Frank, who is one of the non-English co-ordinators. These classes are considered non-English classes and we are to receive special help each week from Miss Frank on language improvement. This includes special rexographed sheets which the children can use, descriptive material such as flannel boards, stages, little figurines, various toys, models of buildings, cars, trucks, people, occupations. The purpose is to strengthen the language of our children within our class, strengthen their concept of the English language, help them to express themselves, how to be understood, and how to understand the teacher and other English-speaking people with whom they are in contact.

Our first meeting had taken place two weeks ago. It was a rather brief meeting to find out exactly what we thought Miss Frank could do for us. At the time, most of us didn't know where we needed help or what we should even ask for. Therefore we had a meeting this week with her, during one of our lunch hours. It was Wednesday, in Miss Frank's office. She gave us different rexograph sheets concerning the unit we are to start Monday on community helpers, and told us that she thought we should highlight the policeman and the fireman. She gave each of us a set of wooden figurines showing the various community helpers—the fireman, the policeman, the nurse, the doctor, the teacher, a milkman—so that we could use these materials to illustrate for the children exactly what the words mean and what they refer to. She gave us rexograph sheets with written descriptions underneath the picture. Some of these will have to be adapted for the slower classes, I know, especially for mine, or the children will not be able to read the material.

The pictures are very explicit. The first picture starts out with: How do we help? How do we help in the classroom? There were some pictures of our worksheet and of the different jobs. The questions ask: Who is the eraser of the boards? Who is the board washer? Who takes the messages around? They start out with how we help, what helping actually is. Then they move out into the bigger cities and ask: Who helps us to get through our daily lives? Who collects the garbage? Who protects us from bad people?

We have a series of about eight such rexograph sheets which Miss Frank had run off for us, which we didn't have to draw up and have run off ourselves.

She also gave us about three or four books each, which we could use during our literature time. Among them were *I Want to Be a Fireman* and *The Policeman and the Fireman*. The books have very good illustrations that I think will hold the children's interest. These books were all in excellent condition. Nothing seemed to have been hanging around years and years. She also has sets of huge pictures showing the community helpers which we could put on our bulletin boards. She also has a planning book, which she said we could follow to make our own plans. However, it is a little

The Rexograph Machine

bit too detailed for some of our classes, but it's good for getting ideas, especially in presenting the children with questions which are interesting to them, and presenting the questions that have been tested and found effective in working with such a unit.

So we all felt that at least the need in our class is being recognized by the school, at least by the N.E. co-ordinator, and that she was willing to give us all the help that she can possibly give. She's always available. She's come into the room several times asking what we want. Of course, this is a little difficult since most of us don't know what we should want at this point and that is why she is providing us with material. She did provide pictures for Columbus Day, a picture of a ship to be colored by the children so we didn't have to spend time making one up. I find that this is very helpful and certainly have gained a very good feeling concerning the help which is available, at least in this one area of improvement of language, which of course ties in with the material which will be available for instruction in reading. It is important to have physical materials in the school which we can use to gain the children's interest in learning to read.

November 2. The most important thing that happened to me in my school this week concerned a certain message which was directed to all the teachers and posted in the principal's office. I think it was important to all of us and it made many of us think and wonder exactly where the independence of the teacher is and how she is being dictated to.

Previous to an announcement which was placed in the office, the teachers had been permitted to rexograph as much material as they wanted for use with the children. Because of the language problem in the school, many of the books are not adequate or not applicable to the situations which are familiar to the children. Therefore much work is done by the teacher in composing her own reading material or experience material, material with reference to the things that the children can grasp in order to gain the same concepts other schools would teach in the second-grade level.

However, about a week and a half ago, an announcement was made over the public address system that from that day on, any rexographed material which was to be run off by a teacher was to have one copy of the material placed in a certain box for the principal. This directive was followed by the teachers and then in the middle of last week, a posted notice was put up in the office and an announcement was made over the public address system to make sure that the notice was read. The notice said that an investigation had been carried on in the school to check on the type of material that was being run off by the teachers and how much paper was being used. Whoever was doing the investigating came to the conclusion that much of the material is useless, especially in certain areas such as art, which in many cases the teachers have combined with social studies or the unit on community helpers which the second-grade non-English classes have been working on. Many of the papers that have been run off show pictures of the community helpers to be colored by the children, and there is usually a brief story underneath with a few words that the children can learn before they work on the actual coloring. However, there was a remark made that if we checked our Art Curriculum Bulletin put out by the Board of Education, there is a statement that this is not creative work. Copy material is not considered art work and therefore it is not to be used, and the announcement said that in the future any rexographed material which was to be done by teachers was to be okayed by the principal before it could be run off for the day. It would have to go through a procedure of receiving okays. There was also a statement as to how we would be checked on how much paper was being used.

Many of the teachers made remarks that since we couldn't get materials in school, that maybe next year they would be asking us to bring our own tables and chairs and books. They felt that this rexographing of materials was a little matter that was blown up into a state by the administration that made many of the teachers feel that they weren't being permitted to think for themselves, that it was taking time on their part and effort on their part to run off the masters and then to run these off into sheets for the children. They certainly wouldn't be creating work which would be evaluated as worthless, something that the children wouldn't gain by. So this is the major important thing and has caused quite a bit of discussion among the teachers, especially the new teachers that I have been in contact with.

DISCUSSION

According to the classical approach to administration, with its emphasis upon scientific management, the most efficient organization is the one which proves to be the most satisfying by virtue of its efficiency. The scientific management school emphasizes an institutional structure with clearly delineated division of labor, a table of organization in which positions are occupied by specialized personnel, and a line of authority which is arranged hierarchically and whose source is a central administration. According to scientific management theories, workers in formal organizations were primarily motivated to perform their various functions by economic rewards. Following this school, early students of administration stressed such factors as rate of pay, physical working conditions, and clear-cut definition of job role, subject to control from higher authority, to keep the institution functioning smoothly and efficiently to fulfill the goals of the institution.[1]

In *Education and the Cult of Efficiency*, Raymond S. Callahan has traced the effects of the scientific management school in the training of school administrators, which stressed emphasis upon organization, plant utilization, and directed authority from a central source.[2]

It was not long, however, before students of institutions became increasingly aware that much of scientific management training in administration was based upon the way in which institutions ought to function rather than upon the way in which they actually did. In addition, scientific management did not, in effect, preclude conflict. Members of the institution, as individuals and as groups, did not accept conveniently without friction and protest the definitions of job

[1] Frederick W. Taylor, *Scientific Management*, New York: Harper & Brothers, 1911.
[2] Raymond S. Callahan, *Education and the Cult of Efficiency*, Chicago: University of Chicago Press, 1962.

roles and production schedules laid out for them. The persistence of industrial conflict served notice that scientific management theories were inadequate to keep institutions functioning efficiently and effectively to fulfill the goals set by the organization. Scientific organization by itself was clearly inadequate to ensure high productivity and worker satisfaction.[3] As far as schools were concerned, scientific management training for administrators de-emphasized professional educational leadership in the schools.[4]

Out of the pioneering work of such scholars as Elton Mayo, John Dewey, Kurt Lewin, F. J. Roethlisberger, and W. J. Dickson, R. Lippitt, and R. K. White, the human relations school of administration developed. As a result of the highly significant studies of what really took place in the institutional world of work, it was found that many factors, outside of economic reward and actual physical conditions of work—which were found to present a wide range of tolerance by workers—were operative in determining efficiency in terms of institutional goals. These were factors primarily concerned with the non-formal or informal social relations between people within institutions.[5]

The studies which have led to the founding of the human relations school came to the conclusions that social factors were primarily responsible for determining the productivity and general efficiency of institutions. Among the findings was that workers react to management and its norms and rewards as groups rather than as individuals. It also stressed that lesser specialization is often more efficient than higher specialization. As a result of these studies several other factors came now to be emphasized in administration. Among these was the need for management to provide for communication channels to be kept open between the various ranks in the

[3] Amitai Etzioni, *Modern Organizations,* Englewood Cliffs, N.J.: Prentice-Hall, 1964, pp. 25–31.
[4] Callahan, op. cit.
[5] Among these were: F. J. Roethlisberger and W. J. Dickson, *Management and the Worker,* Cambridge: Harvard University Press, 1939; and R. Lippitt and R. K. White, "An Experimental Study of Leadership and Group Life," in G. E. Swanson, T. M. Newcomb, and E. L. Hartley (Eds.), *Readings in Social Psychology,* New York: Holt, 1952, pp. 340–55.

organization to provide for exchange of information and feedback. Also, the human relations school pointed to the necessity of involving employees in decision-making.

It was found, too, that non-authoritarian leadership, i.e., democratic leadership of a sort that encouraged an atmosphere of participation and communication, as well as an atmosphere which expressed concern for people, not only concern for work, and which displayed an atmosphere of interest and fairness, provided the best setting for increased efficiency.[6] In other words, the human relations school was predicated on the theory that if people in an organization are happy because within it are provided the organizational structure and congenial atmosphere for participation and mutual understanding, then that organization, rather than one predicated on scientific management, with its lack of concern for people and their social groupings and interactions, would be the most efficient one in terms of institutional goals.

Happy relations among the members of the staff do not necessarily make it possible for the organization to fulfill its goal. Thus, in some "happy" schools, where relations among staff members are pleasant, and where good human relations techniques for communication, participation in decision-making, and democratic leadership are practiced, the children still do not learn and the educational goals of the institution are not met. It is also true that not always can tensions and strains be avoided; these are at times inevitable. They are inevitable because any institution is not just a conglomeration of groups of happy people, but rather they are composed of many groups who may or may not share common interests and values, and who are at times in inevitable conflict with one another. They do not all necessarily accept a common goal, nor are they as groups necessarily willing to forego special interests, or needs, to others competing for power or control.

For these reasons, among others, many recent students of administration have come to question the reality of the human relations approach. The primary disagreement is involved with the awareness that some conflict is inevitable and

[6] Lippitt and White, op. cit.

that conflict ought not to be looked upon as something to be avoided at all times, but rather that conflict appears to have value and can even operate to improve the functioning of the institution. Conflict can operate this way, because it serves to expose areas of disagreement, it may help to establish unity and cohesion where it has been threatened by hostile or antagonistic feelings, it frequently helps to revitalize existing norms, or it contributes to the development of or emergence of new norms, thus acting as a mechanism for adjustment of norms adequate to new conditions. Indeed, it has been suggested that where conflict is smothered, a useful warning system is eliminated, thereby maximizing the danger of catastrophic breakdown.[7]

The techniques developed by the human relations school of administration contribute a great deal to enable administrators to resolve or prevent potential conflict within their institutions. The point must be made, however, that some conflict remains inevitable and will not be eliminated without some internal adjustments, some changes in the institution. In addition, it must be emphasized, organizations in which the human relations are superb and all conflict absent can be happy places for those working within them and at the same time wholly inappropriate in terms of needed shifts to accomplish institutional goals.

The case of the rexograph machine is an example of how good human relations administration may help to resolve potential conflict developing between the principal and his new teachers. At the same time the case illustrates the problem that a basic conflict remains present—a conflict between professional and administrative authority—which cannot be resolved readily.

The real source of conflict here and potential danger to morale concerns itself with the disagreement between lower-echelon employees, the teachers, and their perception of themselves as professionals with the right to make decisions concerning teaching materials, and the administration, which

[7] George Simmel: *Conflict,* trans. Kurt H. Wolff, New York: The Free Press (Macmillan), 1955; see Etzioni, op. cit., pp. 41–49, for a summary of the literature critical of the human relations school.

does not grant this right but rather considers itself responsible for checking, limiting, and exercising control over what the teacher does. The administration rationalizes its actions in terms of carrying out directives from a higher source, the Board of Education Curriculum Bulletin, by the need for efficiency and economy, and by the assumption of responsibility for decisions necessary to carry out the educational goals of the institution.

The young teacher and her colleagues described here have embarked upon teaching with the perception of the teacher as one with professional status. Professionals in our society are different from others in that their status or position carries with it certain privileges which ordinarily are not held by those occupying non-professional or semi-professional positions. Usually, the work of a professional is autonomous, although he is subject to censure by his peers. He is, however, relatively free in so far as his movements are concerned, and the ultimate responsibility for his actions rests with himself. Thus, for example, a physician might consult with colleagues concerning a diagnosis but must assume responsibility for decisions concerning the course of treatment for a patient under his care. Only gross misconduct or incompetency may bring colleague censure or legal difficulties.

In order for him to reach a degree of competency to enable him to act out the role expected of him, the professional requires extraordinarily long periods of education, usually followed by a period of internship served under other professionals who help to induct him into the status of full-fledged member of the profession. Some professions are concerned with the development of new knowledge; others such as medicine and law also carry with them serious responsibilities concerning life-and-death matters and require that information be kept confidential.

The young teachers have entered teaching thinking of themselves as professionals. In reality, however, the primary school is not a professional organization, but has rather been described as a semi-professional one.[8] It differs from professional organizations in that it requires less training of staff

---

[8] Etzioni, op. cit., p. 87.

people in order to teach—although many teachers eventually do continue their education for many years—it does not deal with matters of life and death, and deals only in part with privileged information, and, also important, it covers the communication of knowledge rather than the development of knowledge, as does the university.

There are several characteristics of the semi-professional organization which are in conflict with the teachers' views of their roles as professionals. As stated above, the professional retains control over the decisions involved in carrying out his job. Here, on the other hand, the teacher is subject to the jurisdiction and control of those in positions of higher rank within the organization, particularly the principal. This is not to say that a degree of autonomy is not practiced by teachers. Nonetheless, the teacher, as a semi-professional, and particularly the beginning teacher with low rank in the status hierarchy within the school, is subject to rather tight control.

The signs of restrictions upon the autonomous action of the teacher are so obvious that they sometimes are not considered. One of the most obvious is the very restriction upon place and time of work. Teachers must sign into and out of school, or punch a time clock, and their location during almost the entire school day is subject to determination by superiors. That they are expected to account for their time and location is learned very early by primary school teachers. But in addition to the physical inhibitions placed on teachers, the teacher, as a semi-professional, finds that she is under constant surveillance by those in positions of administrative authority. She is unable to carry out her duties independently, but must rather submit plans of work weekly or by some other unit as the case may be, fairly regularly. Her administrative superiors will visit her classroom or watch her activities with children outside the classroom. They will make surprise visits or they may make appointments to visit, but they will assume responsibility for judging her performance. Also, teachers can expect to have to account for their actions. They may have to report to superiors on why certain actions were taken, and, in addition, the administrative authorities are in the position of correcting the teacher, requiring that correction be followed.

In reality, these beginning teachers are not professionals in

The Rexograph Machine

the full sense of the word. Their training, for one reason or another, has obviously not been intensive enough, or lengthy enough under the tutelage of professionals, as interns to enable them to assume full responsibility for the work they are doing. It is important to recognize that the teachers themselves are aware of this. For this reason they turn to the non-English co-ordinator and respond positively to the advice and concern for their need evinced by this person who is in the position of professional adviser to the teachers. However, the beginning teachers, while recognizing their deficiencies, regard themselves as *developing* professionals, and they view the co-ordinator with good feeling. It comes as a shock to them to find they are not treated as developing professionals by the principal. How can the difference in response to the co-ordinator, as opposed to their response to the principal, be explained?

There are several significant differences between the co-ordinator and the principal, in regard to their relationship to the teachers, that can be explored to answer this question. One of these has to do with sex; the co-ordinator is a woman, the principal is male. Another concerns itself with a basic difference between professional authority and administrative authority, and a third deals with a basic difference in leadership style displayed by the co-ordinator and the principal.

How significant the factor of sex is in this situation is extremely difficult to determine. However, for a variety of reasons, men are playing an increasingly large role in the administration of American elementary schools. Women tend to remain in teaching or in staff positions related to special functions in regard to teaching, rather than seeking advancement through the administrative route. Whether or not this is related to the possibility that those individuals who are less concerned with the professional aspects of the teaching function tend to separate themselves out into the administrative ranks and are thereby less professionally oriented is a matter for further investigation. In addition, as recent study of executive professional leadership in schools by Gross and Herriot has suggested, the sex of the principal is a factor which appears to influence the professional leadership exerted by school heads, women tending to be more professionally oriented than men.[9]

This difference in authority presents a problem despite the fact that those in positions of administrative authority might also be highly knowledgeable, skilled individuals. Indeed, the scientific management school tended to accept an automatic connection between high rank and superiority of merit and experience, giving those people in high positions not only power but also the authority to issue commands, to direct those in subordinate relationship to them. The difficulty which the assumption presents, however, is the fact that achievement of high rank is dependent upon factors other than professional skill, and many of the most highly trained, the experts who enable organizations to fulfill their tasks, are not at the head of the administrative hierarchy, or indeed not even in the regular line of command, but tend rather to be in the middle ranks and outside the regular chain of command. Thus, every organization has its specialists, its experts who have no administrative authority but whose authority stems primarily from the knowledge they have.

The difference between administrative authority and professional authority has been described as necessarily incompatible. Etzioni has stated this very clearly:

Students of the professions have pointed out that the autonomy granted to professionals who are basically responsible to their consciences (though they may be censured by their peers and in extreme cases by the courts) is necessary for effective professional work. Only if immune from ordinary social pressures and free to innovate, to experiment, to take risks without the usual social repercussions of failure, can a professional carry out his work effectively. It is this highly individualized principle which is diametrically opposed to the very essence of the organizational principle of control and coordination by superiors—i.e., the principle of administrative authority. In other words, the ultimate

[9] Neal Gross and Robert E. Herriot, *Staff Leadership in Public Schools, a Sociological Inquiry,* New York: John Wiley & Sons, 1965.

> *justification for a professional act is that it is, to the best of the professional's knowledge, the right act. He might consult his colleagues before he acts, but the decision is his. If he errs, he still will be defended by his peers. The ultimate justification of an administrative act, however, is that it is in line with the organization's rules and regulations and that it has been approved directly or by implication—by a superior rank.*[10]

Thus, in the case of the rexograph machine, the co-ordinator was seen to have behaved as a professional adviser, as one who maintained a senior colleague relationship to the teachers. She did not approach the teachers as one with power within the administrative hierarchy, as she really does not have this position at all. Her authority does not stem from administrative rank but rather from her expertise in the professional problems involved in the teaching of children who have special language difficulties in regard to the use of English. She has demonstrated her competency to the new teachers by preparing materials and lessons which they have recognized as having value. Important too is the fact that she does not command the teacher to employ the teaching aids she has prepared. Rather, treating the new teachers as inexperienced colleagues, she has presented them with guides and suggestions, subject to their revision, leaving the ultimate decisions concerning use in their hands.

The co-ordinator has, in addition, left open lines of communication so that teachers could come to her for consultation concerning problems with which they would like some assistance. It is interesting that she has not waited for these teachers to raise the questions—for as they themselves say, "At that time, most of us didn't know where we needed help or what we should ask for." The co-ordinator instead has proceeded to provide assistance but in a way which has led the teachers to feel that her authority was based on knowledgeability and that she regarded them with respect as developing professionals. "She's always available. She's come into the room several times asking what do we want. Of course,

[10] Etzioni, op. cit., p. 87.

this is a little difficult since most of us don't know what we should want at this point and that is why she is providing us with material."

Thus, the co-ordinator has not commanded or issued directives, controlled, or operated to inspect and judge the new teachers. She has left the teachers with the implication that as they themselves develop expertise they will be better able specifically to request materials and teaching help they consider necessary. Also, there is the implication that the teachers will increasingly be in a position to develop their own materials. Most important is the feeling on the part of the teachers that the ultimate decisions remain theirs.

But what happens as the teachers begin preparing their own materials? They run into conflict with the school administration, whose interference they resent.

In this instance, the administration has issued a directive concerning the limitation of rexographing and also decreed that the materials being rexographed are educationally worthless. This decision has not been reached on the basis of an evaluation of the materials made by the teachers themselves in conjunction with the advice of professionals whose expertise they respect, but rather on the basis of reference to higher authority—a Board of Education curriculum bulletin. The decision has been reached by people in positions of administrative authority in relation to the teachers who, by virtue of the authority gained from high rank within the organization, are in a position to tell the teachers what they can or cannot do.

The decision was based upon a review of materials submitted by the teachers. They had been ordered to submit the materials via the impersonal channel of the public address system, an arm of administrative authority; the conclusion that much of the rexographed material being produced was useless was made *for* them by persons who did not stand in professional authority in relation to them, and finally, they were informed that a future check would be kept on what and how much paper they would use. Thus, efficiency, and economy, administrative concerns in the form of control over the amount of paper being used, and not purely educational criteria were being applied to the rexographing of materials.

The Rexograph Machine

As a result of these events, the teachers, perceiving themselves as professionals, began to wonder "where the independence of the teacher is and how she is being dictated to." Also, they concluded ". . . that they weren't being permitted to think for themselves."

An interesting complication is the fact that principals in positions of high administrative authority are often themselves highly knowledgeable in the various areas of professional concern of the school. Principals have usually been teachers themselves, and often, though not necessarily, bring a great deal of experience and scholarship to their positions. That this combination exists helps to explain the coincidence of administrative and professional authority exerted by some school heads. However, several factors exist which operate to modify or even remove professional authority from the principal. Among these are such matters as his training for the position, which often stresses administration study; the possibility that those least concerned with professional matters separate themselves out into administration channels of advancement; and, perhaps most important, the unreality of expecting one or a very few individuals in administration within a school to have the monopoly on expertise in a wide variety of areas concerning the teaching of children. In any event, ordinarily, the authority exerted by a principal in his school stems from the high rank which the status holds, rather than from his personal knowledgeability in professional matters, for the rank still carries with it authority within the organization.

Now it may very well be that an examination of the rexographed materials by knowledgeable professionals would prove some of them to be of questionable educational value for the children. This is not a point that can be argued here. What is significant, however, is that the decision was being made *for* the teachers without regard for their professional integrity or development. As such, the handling of this matter by the principal was viewed with serious misgivings on the part of some of the teachers. Here they were, confronted point-blank, in rather exaggerated form, with a situation which made it clear to them that they were bureaucratic functionaries. That this has led to strained relations and dissatisfaction is quite understandable.

In a discussion of the effects of bureaucratic organization of the schools upon the educative process, Solon Kimball has made the point that the supervisory system as we know it, based upon position in the hierarchy of the bureaucracy, may defeat the goals of our educational enterprise, the development of the individual creativity and autonomy upon which the continuation of our complex, mobile, and dynamic society depends. It is interesting that the teachers were individualizing their approach with their classes. After being stopped by the administration, it is unlikely that they will feel encouraged to continue to do so. As Kimball points out:

Industrial research suggests to us that it is not the task, however difficult or onerous, that contributes to worker malaise—for work can be a challenge or it can be endured—but that it is the sometimes unbearable weight of a supervisory system which restricts the autonomy and creativeness of the individual. This insight should give us pause, for in the educational hierarchy teacher and pupil are at the bottom of the system; they are the recipients, not the originators, of the messages which flow along the line of command.[11]

The co-ordinator and the principal have also exhibited a different style of leadership, which also contributes to the teacher's feelings about these people. The co-ordinator employed a democratic style of leadership, whereas the principal has acted in an authoritarian manner. With the co-ordinator as leader, the teachers have been free to initiate proposals, consult, and also, provision has been made for meetings—keeping channels of communication between the teachers and the co-ordinator open. In the case of the principal, these factors have not been present and the teachers feel as if they were being dictated to.

It may be that a change in leadership style by the principal would lead to improved relations. It must be pointed out,

[11] Kimball, Solon T., "An Anthropological View of Social System and Learning," in Esther Lloyd-Jones and Esther M. Westervelt, eds., *Behavioral Science and Guidance, Proposals and Perspectives*, New York: Bureau of Publications, Teachers College, Columbia University, 1963, pp. 11–30.

however, that this will not change the fact that administrative authority in the school is at times bound to be in conflict with professional authority, and teachers ordinarily have to obey administrative directives. Better human relations may lessen the tensions and improve relationships, but full professional status for the teachers is still precluded within the present structure of the large inner-city school. A wide range of teacher reaction is possible to this. Those who find the actual position of the semi-professional incompatible with their view of their role as professional may move out or find ways, particularly with increased experience and competency, to function fairly independently anyway. Another possible reaction is acceptance of administrative subservience. A wide range of adjustment is possible, and all teachers must make one or another accommodation to the reality of semi-professional status.

Improved human relations approach by the principal, by keeping open channels of communication, by involving the teachers in an examination, evaluation, and self regulation of rexographed materials, may serve to lessen the developing tensions in this school. Although administrative and professional goals may coincide, basic disagreements may continue to exist where administrative versus professional decisions are in conflict with each other. Yet conflict need not be considered totally negative in effect. Teachers' disagreements with administration, if understood, examined professionally, and the results presented to higher sources responsible for directives, may be useful in indicating needed readjustment in curriculum in the light of the needs of the children and school. For all educational decisions to be directed solely from above lends itself to the dangers of being out of touch with the realities of the problems faced by teachers. It also ignores the necessity for participation by the actors in the educational process.

CHAPTER 9

Bypassed or the Art Lesson

Having passed from a period of "culture shock" through increased familiarity with her class, the teacher is in an excellent position to interpret the behavior of the children to others. However, as in the following case, she is at times bypassed by the principal, treated as help, particularly in maintaining order, rather than consulted as a professional in the analysis of problems confronted by the class.

**Miss Devans
Grade 3/2**

October 26. One of the most important things happened just yesterday when the principal came into my room. She has been coming in quite often, in my estimation, considering that there is no assistant principal in the school and the administrative duties of the school largely rest upon her shoulders. She came in this Friday morning. It was about 9:10 and I was taking attendance with the children. We were all working out the attendance on the bead frame and she asked me if she could take over the class for a moment and she proceeded to lecture them on their behavior at Art the previous day.

The previous day we had had an art period under the instruction of Mr. Long, and during this time, Miss Roth, the principal, had come up and watched what was going on in

Bypassed or the Art Lesson

the art room. Mr. Long, the voluntary art teacher in our school, was giving them a lesson—it's the first time he's doing it and this was my class's second time at art since the beginning of the year. Supposedly we were to go every Thursday, but every Thursday something or other came up. For instance, one Thursday we had our trip, the other Thursday I guess we were tested, another Thursday a visitor came into my room. Each Thursday something else came up, so this was only the second time that the children had an art lesson.

Watching Mr. Long during the art period was quite interesting to me because he is also a beginning teacher. He is attending college and many of the things which he did—only now, because I am teaching, not a student teacher—seemed to mean a lot more to me. For example, in his manner of speaking to the children, I found him doing the same thing that I had done during the first week of school, that is, speaking way above their heads. For example, he would say, "Put your paint on the pallet."

These children don't know what a pallet is, so there was mass confusion in the room. The children were putting their paints in the grooves in the easel. Some of them were placing them on the table, some of them were putting them in the jars. They were trying to do what he said except they didn't know what he meant by what he said.

Then he would say, "Take the brush with the thickest bristles," and again there was confusion because nobody knew what the "thickest bristles" meant. At this point Miss Roth walked in while the children were trying to follow his instructions, not knowing exactly what was meant by them. Only one girl, Bernice Gould, knew what was going on and Miss Roth asked me if I could help him in disciplining the children.

But at this point Mr. Long's nerves were on edge. He said that he had worked with another third grade this morning and that they had been able to master everything. I pointed out to him that this third-grade class that he spoke of was the first third grade on my grade level. The majority of those children were much more fluent in English. There are very few Spanish-speaking children in that class. But he kept telling my children how they couldn't follow instructions and hollering at them and I saw in him many of the things that I had done before. For example, he didn't realize that it wasn't a deficiency in the children themselves but an inability of the teacher to understand that what he was doing was not comprehended by the children. Also, this ranting and raving afterward that Mr. Long did, I have done in my classroom, I will admit. When you're trying to get your point across and it's not understood, you become frustrated and defeated because you plan to teach certain things and nobody understands you. Instead of, when the class gets under control, assuming a calm attitude and not insulting them for their deficiency, you feel defeated and so you keep up this negative approach which is really very bad because the children can never get on their feet. You're insulting their intelligence and the negative doesn't really produce much results.

Anyway, when the principal walked into the art room, there was mass bedlam in the room. She told the class to listen to Mr. Long and they were trying to, but throughout the period there was confusion. She had to leave and she left. While she was still there, there was still confusion.

Mr. Long spoke to me after class and said to me that he would no longer take my class. This is a voluntary thing on his part and he said that they caused him too much trouble and he didn't want them any more. The next day Miss Roth came in to lecture to my class about their behavior at art period, and she told them that Mr. Long would come down to our own classroom the next week—we had been going to a special art room—to give them a lesson with crayons, and if they proved that they could listen to him and follow his instructions that perhaps he could allow them to go back up to the art room. Well, I guess Miss Roth convinced him to give the children another chance, at least in our room. I'm going to have to help him along. I'm supposed to do this and I'll try. The next time he comes I'm going to speak to him about gearing the lesson down to the children's level, using very simple language to express the same concepts.

DISCUSSION

The young woman teacher of this class has described, without using the vocabulary of anthropology, the symptoms of culture shock expressed by the art teacher. He has responded with a degree of hysteria—shouting, confusion, etc.—to his inability to understand the cues in the class environment, the strange behavior of the children, which he and the principal interpret as a threat to himself. The class's own teacher has already recovered from her initial culture shock and is able, better than the others, to understand the true significance of the children's behavior.

Disorder and behavior which appears threatening to authority were treated by this principal as irresponsibility on the part of the children, and subject to reprimand on her part. The children in this case, however, have an advocate, someone who can interpret their behavior accurately and sympathetically and is concerned with their progress and protection in school. Their teacher, having been in a position to observe the genesis of their apparently disruptive actions, and still unsocialized by the school to project all blame for behavioral problems onto the children, has perceptively diagnosed the cause to have been the lack of communication between the art teacher and the boys and girls. Identifying with her young charges, whom she has learned to know, she is impelled to defend them, and makes an effort to understand what the problem is about.

It is interesting that the principal, while she may later seek for causes and solutions, initially responds by attacking the youngsters, berating them for not maintaining decorum and respect for the young art teacher in the room. Now, it may be quite possible to train youngsters to maintain strict obedience and quiet in the face of strange and incomprehensible directions from the teacher. Yet, would not such responses really make the children appear to be "stupid," or apathetic? By their behavior, the children, rather than simply challenging authority, are making it evident that there is a problem here which requires diagnosis. The children are neither stupid nor are they as yet apathetic, nor even sullenly hostile. They are distressed and their behavior is a signal of that distress. It should be a signal for the art teacher too, who rather than being repelled, had he the understanding and maturity, might have asked wherein the lesson had gone wrong. By attacking the children the principal too has left both them and their teacher with the feeling that their behavior and not the teaching technique and manner requires modification. Such responses, such neglect of the cues which the behavior of the children indicate, present the danger of leading to the suppression of symptoms, and possibly to the later outbreak of more serious inability of the children to learn.

The problem of language herein described is rather clear, for these are children who speak Spanish, and have as yet a limited command of English. But, and this is important to recognize, all children have limited vocabulary, even those children of highly "enriched backgrounds." The very brevity of their lives and their lack of exposure to areas of the culture, with the esoteric vocabulary associated with the various specialties, have to make for a limitation on vocabulary. Much learning in school of subjects, from the simplest to the most advanced, requires an introduction to the vocabulary of the subject, and definitions and meanings associated with it. Chemistry has its vocabulary, as does history, mathematics, anthropology, and even painting. The vocabulary of the children, as indeed of all learners, cannot be assumed by the teacher. Demonstration and explanation of the materials used in the painting lesson would certainly have been appropriate. Language is a part of every subject, and vocabulary is the easiest part of language to teach and learn, providing the teacher is cognizant of the need to include explanation and check on whether or not the children understand, without berating them for their innocence and desire to please.

Administrators cannot be expected to diagnose all such disorderly situations rapidly and accurately. However, an approach which emphasizes inquiry is more likely to arrive at correct analysis of the problem.

Not only has the principal made it clear to the children that they must suppress the confusion they experience, but she has also outlined a role for the teacher. The teacher has

Bypassed or the Art Lesson

been placed in the position of acting as a disciplinarian, and, in addition, her subordinate position within the school hierarchy has been made explicit by the principal's behavior. The teacher was not consulted in a professional manner concerning the events of the art lesson. Instead, she was bypassed and her class "punished." Clearly, her educational role has been defined as one of maintaining order and control over the children at the expense of establishing meaningful communication with them as a prelude to constructive, formal learning.

No formal provision has been made for consultation between the two young teachers and the principal concerning diagnosis of the difficulties encountered by the class during the art lesson. Whether or not informal confrontation by the class teacher with the young art teacher will accomplish desirable results is questionable.

CHAPTER 10

"We Know Better" or Grouping

> The manner in which children are grouped into classes in schools has broad educational, social, and political significance. Changes in policy as regards class placement, if not understood or accepted by lower-echelon employees, run the risk of failure. Further, denigration of the principal and loss of respect for his leadership can result.

Miss Gould
Grade 5/3

October 5. The school secretaries in this school used to make all the class placements. When the new principal came he changed this. Now he makes the placements and he is the one making all the mistakes. He doesn't look at record cards. He just throws a child into a class because, as he said, he doesn't want to have slow children with slow children, intelligent with intelligent, and all the non-English-speaking in one class.

Because of that it's very hard for the teachers to teach, because you don't have a level common to all children. He's the one who happens to be making the mistakes, and that is very bad. I know that when the school secretaries placed the children in classes they looked at the I.Q., past records, then they placed the child accordingly. In schools where it's done that way, if a child doesn't fit he's switched to another class, but in our school it's the principal who is doing this in a very haphazard manner.

DISCUSSION

When American education became committed to mandatory schooling for all, the public schools found themselves confronted with the task of handling millions of children. A logical, though not necessary, outgrowth of the problems raised was a system whereby children were grouped by grade, and, in the larger schools, also grouped within grades into classes arranged according to ability levels. Age, maturity, and special characteristics have also played their part in the grouping process. The new system was a far cry from the one-room rural schoolhouse with its wide variety of age and learning levels under the tutelage of a single teacher.

In order to facilitate an orderly grouping of pupils in the expanding schools of twentieth-century America, various measuring instruments were adopted to help classify pupils. Among these were the relatively crude group Intelligence Quotient tests, and standardized achievement tests, primarily in reading and arithmetic. As these instruments became further refined, they purported to be useful in diagnosis and prediction, but their utilization in mass school systems has been not so much in diagnosis concerning learning disability or need. Rather, they are widely used as administrative instruments to facilitate the sorting of youngsters into groups composed of children tagged with similar test results, i.e., in relatively "homogeneous" learning groups, as opposed to groups deliberately set up as "heterogeneous," i.e., to have in them a sample of the pupil population. Generally, heterogeneous groupings are not made by age, another possible alternative. The notion that children learning together ought to comprise a common age group, with a year or less spread, is the practice in American public schools. Typically, also, heterogeneity of a class by sex rarely bothers teachers, at least on the conscious level. The assumption of the public school is that boys and girls are much the same. The predictive value of the tests may be related to the fact that children are tagged very early in their school careers and differential education is then provided.

Whether or not homogeneous or heterogeneous groupings are superior one to the other in terms of learning by children is a matter that has been widely researched as well as disputed by educators.[1] Although both sides of the argument can be presented, the research evidence does not support the contention that homogeneous groupings provide a superior learning and teaching atmosphere. Much of the argument and research is complicated by the fact that homogeneity and heterogeneity are themselves imprecise concepts, for they are often the function of crude measuring devices, and, in addition, are dependent for definition upon the school population. Thus, for example, classes grouped heterogeneously in a highly selective honors school such as Bronx High School of Science will display a different range of abilities than classes so arranged in a large metropolitan comprehensive high school drawing a very diverse student population. Also, homogeneous groupings in a school with a diversified population can exhibit a wider variety of pupil characteristics than heterogeneous classes in a school with a more homogeneous population. Most educators would agree, too, that the most homogeneous class is also very heterogeneous from the point of view of learning abilities and personality styles within the class.

On the whole, however, in urban schools, and especially as one moves up into the higher grades, heterogeneous classes present a very broad spectrum of achievement levels, as well as behavioral problems, and to the teacher unfamiliar with this arrangement, it seems to pose greater teaching difficulties than do more homogeneously grouped classes. There are several reasons for this. One is related to the fact that where classes are grouped according to test performance, these classes tend to be arranged hierarchically on the grade, in descending order of prestige ranging from the "best" class, the one exhibiting the highest scores, down to the "worst" class. The tests themselves provide a timetable of expected

[1] See Jane Franseth, "Research in Grouping: A Review," *School Life*, Vol. 45, June 1963, pp. 5–6; and Miriam Goldberg et al., *The Effects of Ability Grouping*, New York: Teachers College Press, 1966.

achievement against which each grade is measured, and classes that are below grade in performance are not only viewed as less prestigious for pupil and teacher alike, but also appear to frustrate the teacher's view of how the children should be performing, making her less satisfied with them.

In addition, the lower classes on a grade tend to become the "dumping grounds," for sifted out of the "better" classes are children who exhibit behavioral and emotional problems, children with limited use of English, and children who for many subjective reasons do not win the teacher's approval or recommendation for retention. In addition, strangers, i.e., children who are very recent arrivals to the school and do not bring records of their performance, are likely also to be placed in the lower classes on the grade.

Combined with these factors is the tendency for young, inexperienced teachers, and especially substitutes, to be assigned these classes, many of which take on such labels as "discipline" classes, "adjustment" classes, or just stupid, bad, terrible, or, most contemptuously, "the animals." Teachers who have spent many years in a school avoid assignment to the less prestigious classes and prefer the "better" classes. Of course, this is not always possible, and some years even experienced teachers with some influence in administrative assignment, or in schools where rotation systems are enforced, must assume responsibility for them. But these times are regarded as temporary, and one hopes to be assigned a "better" class next time around.

To place the children of the "poorer" and "better" classes together appears threatening to the teacher who feels that the slow or disruptive child will hold back the others, or that she does not have the skills or curriculum resources to deal with a variety of children who appear so disparate to her. Perhaps more important, it is threatening because it disturbs the traditional way of viewing the children. When the classes are hierarchically arranged, there is also likely to be a hierarchical arrangement of expectation of teacher behavior and expectation of pupil performance.[2] In the "better" classes there

---

[2] See Robert Rosenthal and Lenore Jacobson, *Pygmalion in the Classroom,* New York: Holt, Rinehart & Winston, 1968, p. 114,

is a greater stress on academic achievement, in the "poorer" classes there is a greater stress placed on the maintenance of order and a lower expectation of achievement.[3] The mixture of the two requires a re-evaluation of expectation and attitude.

But wide variety of educational level and the difficulties faced by the teacher unprepared to deal with it represent only one aspect of the problem presented by heterogeneous class placement. More often than not, the arguments that abound about grouping are political and social in nature. Thus, there are those who argue that all Americans must learn to live together and that in school they ought to experience this, the notion being that a more egalitarian school experience will make for a more egalitarian citizenry. Countering this argument is the belief that our society requires an intellectual elite and this in turn requires separate and special education in order to help the nation maintain itself as a world power.

The problem is further compounded by the nature of the social revolution led by the civil rights movement in this country, which is demanding that the black youngster be provided with the same exposure via educational opportunity to the tools for participation along the high social strata of the larger society. The urban poor, white and black, confined to the schools of the inner city, are increasingly restive at the signs that their children face educational failure and thus are limited in their movement through the schools to positions of higher status in the nation.

In urban schools which are becoming or have become desegregated, homogeneous class placement appears to frustrate the goals of integration in that poorly prepared, academically deficient youngsters coming from previously segregated schools are likely to find that they are subject to segregation within desegregated schools because of class placement policies based upon test results. Thus, segregation by race can continue. This is true even where the segregation is accompanied

---

for evidence of how teachers' expectations of children affect the pupils' intellectual development.

[3] G. Alexander Moore, Jr., *Realities of the Urban Classroom*, New York: Doubleday Anchor Press, 1967. Based on Project TRUE observations, this book portrays the different approaches to classes of different status in the urban school.

by sincere efforts by educators to group for the purpose of providing suitable course content and remedial work to raise academic levels. Assignment of black children to bottom classes for whatever reason sometimes appears to those committed to integration to ensure educational failure. On the other hand, heterogeneous class placement without careful and special provision for the problems faced by youngsters with disparate preparations presents other kinds of frustrations.[4]

Social class position is also influential in the matter of grouping. Since children of the middle class appear to give their teachers evidence of better performance by behaving in ways considered appropriate by the teacher,[5] homogeneous grouping can lead to segregation by socioeconomic class, even within *de facto* segregated schools, whether they be all white or all black. Thus, not only do classrooms appear to be homogeneous by mental ability, however crudely measured, but also tend to be homogeneous by social class in schools where the pupil population is drawn from socially diverse population groups. There is a wide variety of reasons for this, including the nature of the tests themselves—which have been closer in content to the experiences of children of more affluent groups—as well as the manners and behavior of the children, pressures of parents, availability of outside assistance to support the children through any difficulties they may have in schools. American schools have traditionally acted as sorting mechanisms in which lower-class and minority group pupils did not fare as well, on the whole, as others.[6]

Grouping practices have further political implications. Where heterogeneity of race, class, and achievement levels do exist in a school population, especially in newly integrated schools, the maintenance of special classes for children viewed as having higher ability, or a tracking system which is a more rigid grouping according to ability, is sometimes de-

[4] Estelle Fuchs, *Pickets at the Gates,* New York: The Free Press (Macmillan), 1966, Ch. 7, "Pupil Grievances," pp. 139–54.

[5] Howard S. Becker, "Social Class Variations in the Teacher-Pupil Relationship," *Journal of Educational Sociology,* Vol. 25, 1952, pp. 451–65.

[6] Robert J. Havighurst and Bernice L. Neugarten, *Society and Education,* 3rd. ed., Boston: Allyn & Bacon, 1966, p. 82.

liberately employed to keep white parents and even middle-class Negro parents from deserting the public school.[7] This is an effort, questionable at best, to allay fears and cater to a desire to maintain distance between the races, or distance between the children of the middle and working class from children of the lower class. Fears also stem in part from the real concern of parents and teachers that without special programing the educational level of the academically oriented children will be drawn downward. The fact that the inner-city school has not been noted for the intellectual challenge and stimulation of its population feeds into this concern.

The most significant thing about grouping is that it helps to define the characteristics and expectation of performance of the children who are labeled by group membership. This labeling frequently takes place very early, and is related to judgments made by kindergarten and first-grade teachers, to results on tests that assume much about the experiences of children and take little account of sex, maturational differences, etc. The early grouping of children has been criticized by educators as well as by social reformers for defining learning roles for children far too early in their academic lives, by marking them off as being the educable as opposed to uneducable, by grouping them into classes that range from the best down to the worst (although in the slum school the entire school takes a position subordinate to the middle-class or suburban school), by creating teacher and school definitions of the abilities of the children before they have been taught, and by providing the children with self-concepts related to school experience.

Recent research has presented evidence that teacher expectation has a profound influence upon the intellectual performance of children. Experiments have indicated that positive expectations on the part of the teacher can lead to improved intellectual performance on the part of children.[8] Policies that restrict the teacher's view of her pupils as being less

---

[7] The Washington, D.C., public school system was an example of this. In the spring of 1967 the tracking system here was legally challenged, and the courts have ruled that official policy must change.

[8] Rosenthal and Jacobson, op. cit.

educable than others feed into a situation in which the prophecy of pupil failure is self-fulfilling.

In response to many criticisms, ranging from those based upon the educational questions concerning the desirability of heterogeneity versus homogeneity for learning, through the ideological arguments concerning the need to avoid internal school segregation by social class or race, new approaches to grouping are being tried. Among these is the ungraded school, in which traditional grade levels have been abandoned and children grouped according to achievement.[9] In New York City, the More Effective School Program, designed to promote superior education in *de facto* segregated slum schools, deliberately chose heterogeneous class placement while maintaining the traditional grade organization.

In the case of "We Know Better," it is clear that the new principal of the school has chosen to institute heterogeneous class placement in a school where homogeneous placement had previously been the rule. Previous to his arrival, children had been grouped according to their scores, a purely administrative procedure handled routinely by the school secretary.

This teacher's comments reflect a serious lack of communication between the principal and his staff as regards his educational philosophy. Here is a principal who does not believe in grouping his pupils homogeneously according to I.Q., reading level, or any other criterion. His staff, on the other hand, or at least the new teacher and those who talk with her, and the school secretary who previous to this principal's appointment handled class placement assume incorrectly that homogeneous grouping is the only educationally valid procedure. To them the principal's behavior appears to be "haphazard," resulting in making all the "mistakes."

There is no way of knowing how carefully this principal planned his heterogeneous groupings. Certainly, true heterogeneous grouping does require careful perusal of records in order to ensure the outcome, and even greater planning than simple grouping by I.Q. or reading score. Nor is there enough

---

[9] Frank R. Dufay, *Ungrading the Elementary School*, West Nyack, N.Y.: Parker Publishing Co., 1966; and B. Frank Brown, "The Non-Graded High School," *Phi Delta Kappan*, Vol. 44, February 1963, pp. 206–9.

known about the degree of his commitment to the educational philosophy behind his method of class placement, and his educational objectives in arranging classes this way. Whether or not his was a superficial response to a policy dictated from higher echelons within the school system administration is also not clear.

It is obvious, however, that the educational philosophy and the educational objectives behind his procedures have not been made clear to the staff, nor is the staff cognizant of any carefully thought through design procedures. Most important to the beginning teacher, pedagogical supports to ensure the successful outcome in learning for the children in heterogeneous classes are seen as unavailable by the teacher. She is fearful and wary of teaching classes composed of children displaying a wide degree of achievement and ability levels as measured by tests, and, it may be assumed, also displaying a wide variety of behavioral characteristics. She has received no briefing concerning expectation of pupil achievement and thus retains the prejudicial view that the group I.Q. score is prognostic, a view which prejudges the children and may influence her behavior toward them. Yet there is no evidence that curriculum planning, consultation concerning methods, feedback, and evaluation are taking place to take into account the changed character of class placement in the school.

The absence of these supports raises an issue very much related to the problem of affecting change in bureaucratic organizations. On the whole, bureaucratic organizations appear designed to maintain stability and continuity.[10] They are often conservative and slow to change. Yet, in order to function effectively within a given cultural context, bureaucracies must undergo some adjustment as the world about them changes. Excessive rigidity is disadvantageous to the organization. Urban school systems have been slow to respond to the new social requirements that they provide increased and improved academic education to larger numbers of lower-class and minority group pupils, to prepare them for a world of

[10] For discussions on the nature of bureaucracy see Robert K. Merton et al., eds., *Reader in Bureaucracy,* Glencove: Free Press, 1952; and Peter Blau, *Dynamics of Bureaucracy,* Chicago: University of Chicago Press, 1955.

"We Know Better" or Grouping

work resulting from accelerated automation and increased urbanization. This is bound up not only with the need to educate for a world that values technological skills and can afford to maintain huge numbers of unproductive young people for the periods of time required for advanced learning, but also to incorporate the Negro who is demanding his full share of equal access to participation in the larger society.

Most of the big changes in school organization in recent years have been responses to external stimuli, periods of crisis and conflict, such as the launching of Sputnik by the U.S.S.R. and the dramatic boycotts and protests led by the civil rights movement.[11] However, there are times when the leadership of a bureaucratic organization is quite willing and ready to institute change. But directives issued from the leadership are not in themselves guarantees of successful carrying out of new programs. Students of bureaucratic organization have shown that this is due to the fact that lower-echelon personnel have a tendency to continue functioning as they have always done. More specifically, where lower-level functionaries do not accept the change, or do not believe it to be realistic or practical, they can effectively prevent the effectiveness of the new program.[12] This is due sometimes in part to their not carrying out the directives. At other times it can be the result of pressure exerted to convince the leadership to change its plans.

In order to achieve real change, there must be understanding, acceptance, and commitment in the lower ranks. Structural or ideological changes, each standing alone, are not enough; they must operate together. At the same time, changes directed from above must be accompanied by the resources to assist those who are required to carry out the program and are lacking in the skills to do so. Where these conditions do not hold, there is real danger that the policy change may fail.

In this case there are grounds for honest dispute concerning the value and implications of heterogeneous versus homogeneous grouping of children. More thorough planning and consultation with his staff may not achieve complete support for

[11] See Lewis Coser, *The Functions of Social Conflict*, New York: The Free Press, 1956.
[12] Seymour M. Lipset, *Agrarian Socialism*, Berkeley and Los Angeles: University of California Press, 1950, pp. 255–75.

the new organizational policy instituted by the principal. It would, however, remove the principal from the position of being viewed as incapable and deliberately negligent. It would also expose the difficulties and fears perceived by teachers, so that they might be resolved. Similarly, the policy needs exploration and study with interested community groups and the parents, for it has implications for them as well.

Ignorance on the part of the staff concerning the rationale behind his directives leads to denigration of the principal and loss of respect for his leadership. Even worse, it can lead to effective failure of any policy change designed to better the education of the children, for directives issued from above do not by themselves ensure change.

CHAPTER 11

Exploited

Work assignments that run contrary to a teacher's conception of her role and educational norms can lead to inhibition of her productive contribution to the school.

Miss Gould
Grade 5/3

December 12. My least successful lesson this week was quite disheartening. I am in charge of the music in the assembly. This Tuesday I went down to the auditorium all prepared to teach the assembly the "Star-Spangled Banner," the first stanza of "America," and I would have loved to have done a round with the children to "Row, Row, Row Your Boat." First we had the color guard come down, and then it was time to sing the "Star-Spangled Banner," and we sang it. Then afterward I got up in front of the assembly, and I started to teach "Star-Spangled Banner," because half of the auditorium had learned it last year, but the other half had never learned the words, and so it was my job to teach it to them.

All of a sudden, as I was teaching, I saw all the teachers get up and leave the auditorium. I didn't know what had happened. All of a sudden I was in charge of over two hundred children, and it was just the piano teacher and myself in the auditorium.

Of course, the children got restless and noisy, and it was

impossible to keep them under control. I was disciplining them more than teaching them. Later on I found out that the assistant principal had decided to call a meeting of the fifth- and sixth-grade teachers while their classes were in assembly. I thought this was very unfair, for no one teacher can hold the attention and have control of an auditorium filled with over two hundred children. These children are, on the whole, restless and can't sit still. If their teachers are there, they will pay attention, but if no one is there to curb them, it is utter chaos. And this is just what happened.

I was a wreck after this assembly, and I feel it was my most unsuccessful lesson because nothing was really gained from it. Some of the children repeated the words but most of them did not. Half of them were not listening, and when I tried to do the round, all I got was shouting, and it was a complete failure. This, of course, was not entirely my fault. Any teacher, no matter how experienced she is, would have difficulty in controlling such a large group of children without any help whatsoever. . . .

When I saw the principal this week he mentioned to me the fact that he had gone to a meeting with the other principals of the district. And he told me that the other principals were bragging about the fact that they have a glee club. He then told me he would like for me to organize a glee club in this school. Actually, I really have no time to do this; I told him that my class is more important to me right now—I was behind in work—but he wouldn't listen. He said that there's no reason why we couldn't have a glee club, and why I couldn't have time to work with the children of the fifth and sixth grades.

What he doesn't seem to understand is that my children need me; they cannot be left on their own to do work on their own. They need help at all times, because there is always someone who does not understand what is going on. I intend to speak to him again on this, because besides my class needing me, I have never led a group before. I don't even know where to begin, and on top of that, he wants me to do it *a cappella,* which is without accompaniment, and I can barely read notes, which would make it harder for me to relate to the children.

Also, I spoke with Mr. Louis, the assistant principal. He

Exploited

came in to see me after the assembly, and it was quite ironic, for I had just scolded my class because they had been making noise in the assembly and he proceeded to praise them! He also talked to me about late passes and lateness. The children who come late are detained downstairs until they get a pass which permits them to enter the classroom. This isn't a bad idea, except that the children who are detained don't get upstairs until 9:30, by which time they have missed a half hour's work even though they have come to school before nine o'clock.

I had explained this to the assistant principal and he said he would try to improve the situation but the lines are too long. He told me I should lecture the children on lateness but I would have to abide by the rules and not let the children in without passes.

My biggest problem with the assistant principal is that he insists on calling me by my first name in front of the children. Not only in front of my class, but in front of the whole assembly. Now, the children hear this and they definitely pick it up, because one child has already said something in regard to my first name. And I really don't know how to go about telling the assistant principal tactfully that you just don't call teachers by their first names in front of their classes. To cite an example, the microphone once kicked back some juice in the assembly, and the assistant principal, at the top of his voice, yelled down to me, "Lucy, pull out the plug." All the children were hysterical and amazed. This is something that could have been avoided. I find that I don't have as yet enough courage to tell the principal and the assistant principal how I feel. As far as the principal is concerned, I don't want to do the glee club, but I don't know how to get out of doing it.

During the week, I've seen them and they've asked me how my class was. The principal asked me if I had done any work on the glee club. All in all, though I hate to say this, I try to avoid them as much as possible. I find the less I see of these two men, the better off I am. . . .

January 11. As far as the principal and the assistant principal sometimes taking advantage of the teachers and myself, I'd like to give three examples. First of all, there is one teacher who just came into the school this year, Miss Smith, and somehow or other the principal found out that Miss Smith was a professional dancer at one time. This was a big mistake on her part, to let him know this. I don't know if she did or not, but what happened was he told her he wanted her to start a dancing class for the children after school, of course without being paid, and that she would have to be responsible for a program in dancing for the assembly. This was an example of how the principal takes advantage of the teachers.

Another example is Mrs. De Peuw, who is my buddy teacher and was my co-operating teacher last term. She also is given an awful lot of assignments. She has special course work in library, so she is given the job of ordering all the books for the library and taking care of the library when the librarian is not there. She also, being a very good teacher and being able to get the most out of her children, was given the added responsibility of the science fair. In other words, she is completely in charge of the science fair and has to make sure that everything is going according to what is expected.

Now, as far as I am concerned, I am in charge of the music assembly and the glee club. My principal went to a meeting with other principals at the superintendent's office and he heard other principals talking about a good glee club, so he figured he had to have one to show off too, and I am not kidding, this is just how he feels. Everything for him is show, so he came to me and he insisted in quite harsh words that I have a glee club. Now, I never worked with a glee club before. I didn't know what to do. And besides that, my class is not that bright that they can afford to lose me for an hour.

I was very annoyed over it, but there was nothing I could do, because he insisted and he said he would make it hard for me if I didn't do it. In this respect this is how the principal and the assistant principal as well try to take advantage of the teachers in the school, and this is why many of the teachers who can do other things do not. For example, the principal put up a notice saying that he would like someone who could teach Spanish. Now, I know Spanish, and I wanted to teach Spanish before I went into elementary school teaching, so that I could teach Spanish, but I would never let my principal know that I can even speak Spanish, because that's all I would have to do and I would get that position, which I cannot afford to do.

DISCUSSION

Certainly, individual differences are involved in the willingness or unwillingness of individuals to accept extra assignments in their schools. Some individuals enjoy a wide variety of activity, the excitement of new endeavors, and the development of their own skills and abilities in channels other than classroom teaching. To others, new experiences and responsibilities may represent a threat, create anxiety, and therefore inhibit the willingness of the teacher to attempt new tasks, causing her to retreat to the familiar. Differences in intelligence, experience, and physical energy also affect the response of individuals to new assignments.

Over and beyond the psychological and physical differences between human beings, however, are certain social factors which help explain variations in regard to the assumption of responsibilities. Among these are the validation of the teacher in her new status position, the compatibility of school norms with teacher expectations, and the deference and demeanor accorded individuals within the school.

The new teacher is first of all primarily concerned with establishing a sense of security and identity in her new status, that of teacher. Because of her previous expectations, this usually means successful management and education of the children in the class to which she has been assigned. Success in this area, i.e., satisfactory behavior and learning by her charges, is her way of becoming assured that she is truly a teacher. In addition, she requires evidence from the administration and from her colleagues that she is accepted as well as acceptable in her new position.

In addition to the need to validate her status within the social organization of the school, the teacher is a member of a larger society and brings with her cultural attitudes coming out of the traditions of that society. These traditions include ideas concerning appropriate pupil, teacher, administration behavior as well as generalized views of the school and its functions.

The concepts of what people ought to do, of what they are expected to do under given circumstances, have been termed "norms."[1] For example, part of the Western, industrial tradition is that one ought to do a fair day's work for a fair day's pay (a norm, incidentally, very much in evidence in arguments over welfare payments and guaranteed incomes for the unemployed). Sometimes termed sanctions, these idealized versions of appropriate or expected behavior delimit the boundaries of acceptability. Norms represent ideal behavior. In reality, people behave differently, but too great a departure from the norm subjects one to punishment or social disapproval, whereas conformity, on the other hand, is rewarded.

Norms grow out of the interaction and sentiments of many persons over periods of time. In very general terms, norms concerning schools assume that the function of the school is to enable children to progress in academic skills, and, in our time, these are measured by standardized tests. Variations on particular norms do exist. These grow out of college training, demands of articulate parents, the pressures exerted by diverse groups of pupils, among others. There appears to be a different set of norms concerning academic achievement for affluent suburban schools than for inner-city urban schools. Some writers have even suggested that part of the difficulty faced by inner-city school children is precisely the fact that in accordance with existing norms so little is expected of them in the traditional area of learning.[2] Within schools, too, variations on the norms exist for various classes on the grade.[3]

In addition to concepts concerning how schools ought to function, new teachers are also likely to bring with them cultural attitudes with respect to appropriate and inappropriate

---

[1] See George C. Homans, *The Human Group*, New York: Harcourt, Brace & Co., 1950, p. 123, for a full discussion on norms.

[2] Kenneth B. Clark, *Dark Ghetto*, New York: Harper & Row, 1965, p. 131; also Kenneth B. Clark, "Segregated Schools in New York City," *Journal of Educational Sociology*, February 1963, p. 249.

[3] G. Alexander Moore, *Realities of the Urban Classroom*, Garden City: Doubleday Anchor Books, 1967.

behavior on the part of people filling the various status positions within the school. The teacher is aware of a hierarchy of personnel within the school organization, and thinks of the principal, assistant principal, teachers, children, and parents as occupying different positions in relation to one another, each position carrying with it different roles.

In the case cited, the principal's assignments appear to the teacher as being incongruent with her expectations of what a teacher's role ought to be. The teacher's view of her role may have developed as a result of many factors, including her own observations of teachers as she progressed through school herself, and through expectations developed in the course of her formal preparation for teaching in the university. In order to have reached her position as teacher, she would usually have had a school history of fairly successful academic achievement, and would probably have been assigned, as a pupil, to classes that stressed academic work. In addition, teacher education emphasizes pedagogical objectives, whereas the teacher on the job in a slum school is often confronted with new norms, norms emphasizing the maintenance of order, discipline, keeping records, and, in this case, extracurricular activities she does not see as possible within her schedule.

The teacher is very troubled by the fact that her pupils are not achieving at an academic level which she views as the norm for their grade. To her, her primary responsibility is to work at the task of bringing the pupils to a level of reading performance congruent with the norm. The behavior of the administration appears to her to be ignoring this basic requirement of her role as a teacher. Thus, she is concerned over the prolonged detention of late pupils who then miss instruction, and she is concerned that the glee club assignment will affect the teaching relationship with her class. Also, calling out the fifth- and sixth-grade teachers during the assembly program is seen by her as a cynical disregard for the teaching function of the occasion and as the utilization of her time for baby-sitting, for ". . . nothing was really gained from it."

Compounding the problem for the teacher is the fact that both the principal and the assistant principal do not appear to act in ways considered appropriate by the teacher. Both have departed markedly from her view of good manners. The principal has done this by seeking to impose an unwanted task upon her—". . . he insisted and he said he would make it hard for me if I did not do it." The assistant principal too has violated her view of good manners by calling her by her first name before the children—something that in many school situations is not necessarily inappropriate, but which to this teacher, in the formal school setting, appears highly inappropriate. In addition, his calling a meeting of the teachers during the assembly period without consulting Miss Gould concerning her being left in charge of all the children is seen as ignoring her needs.

Thus, the principal and the assistant principal are seen to have violated the norms concerning behavior appropriate to their position, as well as the norms concerning "good manners." The matter of manners is of significance here because it is through them that the teacher may or may not perceive herself as worthy, and this is very much related to whether or not she is willing to assume responsibilities in the school.

The conduct of persons toward one another in social situations has been analyzed by Erving Goffman.[4] He has discussed in detail the way in which persons have maintained privacy and identity in the face of social contacts that operate to destroy the separateness of the individual. Having derived his sense of self from others, according to Goffman, a person's sense of worth and significance is threatened by his vulnerability and penetrability by social interaction. He speaks of persons as bearers of demeanor and the recipients of deference. By deference is meant "the appreciation an individual shows another to that other." In other words, by deference is meant the image of that individual that others are obliged to express to him in their conduct toward him. All participants in a social situation are involved in the rules of deference. Ordinarily, however, persons in higher positions do have more rights than do persons in subordinate positions. Yet metaphorical boundaries do exist around the self, and, in addition, social norms concerning appropriate behavior attached to each status position do exist.

[4] Erving Goffman, "The Nature of Deference and Demeanor," *American Anthropologist*, Vol. 58, June 1956, pp. 473–502.

Although the assistant principal is in a higher position than is Miss Gould and does have more rights than she, he has behaved in a way viewed as highly inappropriate. The assistant, by calling Miss Gould by her first name in front of the children, particularly in the assembly by shouting, "Lucy, pull out the plug!" seemed to be indicating to her that she was no or little different than the children themselves. This was perceived by the teacher as disrespectful to one in her position, as well as threatening to her relationship with her class, for his behavior was not helping to establish her own position as teacher, superordinate to the children.

Distance between the actor and the recipient in social relationships is essential for defining relationships and for not violating the "ideal sphere which lies around the recipient." Goffman has described the avoidance rituals and presentation rituals employed to establish social distance. Avoidance rituals refer to things one should not do. Appropriate deference on the part of the assistant principal calls for avoidance of calling to the teacher by her first name across an assembly full of children. Presentation rituals are things which should be done to define to recipients how they are regarded. Among these are salutations, compliments, invitations, and services. The principal and assistant principal do not here seem to be paying attention to any of these in their contact with the teacher. A generalized question about how the teacher is getting along with her class does not fill this need. Asking her to assume the leadership of a glee club may under other circumstances indicate a principal's pleasure with a teacher's performance. But the assignment here has not been presented in such a way. The imposition of the task and the comparison with other schools, without stress placed on the educational requirements felt essential by this teacher for the children in her class, served rather both to demean the administration in her eyes and to define the teacher as being "used," as subservient help. Thus the teacher was left feeling exploited.

That element of a person's behavior that sets him up to those in his presence as a person having desirable qualities and thus worthy of respect is demeanor. Demeanor actually represents socially defined "good manners," which are essential to the establishment of basic trust in any relationship.

Again, the administrators in this school have not left the teacher feeling respect for them by their behavior. They have contradicted the norms she had expected and have led her to seek literally to avoid social interaction with them. Avoiding their presence, she says, ". . . the less I see of these two men, the better off I am."

The social behavior of the administration toward Miss Gould has not indicated to her that she is a teacher worthy of respect and dignity in their eyes. On the contrary, the avoidance and presentation rituals practiced or rather not practiced here appear to have left her with the feeling that the administration has overstepped the bounds of propriety. Left with the choice of accepting a loss of individuality and personal subservience to administration uses, or insisting on maintaining privacy and social distance, the teacher chooses the latter by resisting efforts to engage her in extra school activities. Extra responsibilities are viewed by this teacher as indicative of her unworthiness as an individual, as indicative of her willingness to be used by others for their own purposes, purposes not seen as congruent with her view of the function of the school. In addition, extra responsibilities pose added physical and emotional strains to an already overburdened teacher.

Were the activity of glee club leader viewed as having value for the children and/or providing social acceptance for the teacher by the administration and the staff of the school, the teacher might accept more willingly. However, where the activity is viewed as neglect of the children, where the activity is seen not as supportive of the teacher's position but rather as the taking on of jobs others have sloughed off, or in terms of exploitative, opportunistic behavior on the part of the administrator in order to glorify his personal performance without regard to the needs of the teacher or the educational needs of the children, there is bound to be resentment.

Both the principal and the assistant principal in this school have given this teacher the impression that they are really not concerned with nor cognizant of the problems confronted by her in regard to the establishment of her status as a teacher, the learning of reading by her pupils, something which justly concerns her deeply, nor are they aware of her seriousness concerning the teaching of songs in the assembly. Rather than participating and sharing in the assembly occasion to give the beginning teacher the thrill of a successfully carried out singing lesson, they utilize her time as "baby-sitting," as "covering" the children while the other teachers are called out to a meeting. Their behavior is not only viewed by the teacher as exploitative, it also has served to provide a negative experience in her professional development, has served to make her annoyed with the youngsters in her class, and has made her cynical regarding the school administration.

A school atmosphere which allows for the fullest development of the talents of teachers and children is desirable. The assignment of unwilling personnel to activities, in order to go through the mechanics of maintaining activities, is not likely to accomplish this aim. In order for teachers to enthusiastically participate in new programs and activities every effort should be made for the activity to be understood in terms of the norms brought by the teachers where these are positively oriented toward raising the educational level of the children; provision must be included to provide social rewards for the teacher in terms of acceptance by the faculty, the administration, and the children; it must be viewed as non-exploitative in terms of time and energy required, and it must be measured against alternative use of teacher time in the accomplishment of educational and social goals. Adequate attention must be given the deference and demeanor practiced within the school organization to enable individuals to view themselves and others as persons worthy of respect.

The administrators of this school do not appear to have given any of these matters deliberate consideration. Work assignments seem to have grown out of organizational needs rather than out of consideration for the educational requirements of the children. Teacher assignments run contrary to the teacher's expectation of her role. This teacher has been left feeling exploited, abandoned, and cynical, rather than given the feeling of belonging and functioning effectively. The result has been to inhibit her productive contribution to the school.

CHAPTER 12

Who Stole the Cookie Money?

Stealing, or the bringing into schools of objects viewed as frightening or potentially dangerous, is not uncommon. Generally, teachers refer such matters to the administration. How they are handled has serious implications for relations within the school, as well as for relations between school and community.

Miss Kooper
Grade 6/3

October 12. This week there were so many important things. The other day, for example, William Watkins was walking by the wastepaper basket. He wanted to throw something away. The children know that they're not to go to the wastepaper basket; they have to save their garbage, papers, and everything until three o'clock, when the basket goes around. So when I saw him coming up to the basket to throw something away I told him to sit down. Then I saw he had a cigarette in his hand. I said, "William, what is that in your hand?" and he showed me a cigarette. So I said, "Throw it away," and he sat down. Later I said to him, "Where did you get it?" He said he found it on the floor, on the stairs, and he meant to throw it away but he had forgotten. So I let it pass.

There's been another boy also with a pack of cigarettes

Who Stole the Cookie Money?

in his shirt pocket. I'm not quite sure what to do about it. I'll have to speak to Mr. DeVito, the assistant principal, about this, because I don't like the idea of cigarettes in the classroom, and yet I don't think that I can just take them if the kids aren't smoking them or don't have them out openly.

**Miss Brewster
Grade 2/3**

November 23. I had cookie money in my desk and it was stolen. I know that I shouldn't have money in my desk. I should actually keep it in my wallet so that was wrong on my part. These children knew that the money was there before and there were times when I've had more money than I had when it was stolen. I don't know who took it. The children blame Louis Nelson. I sent the matter down to the principal when I found out.

I found the money was missing when I went to sell cookies. That day the money was not in the drawer and I looked through the drawer and it wasn't there. I asked the children where the cookie money was, and they told me that Louis had taken it. Immediately I wrote a note to the principal and he told me that I shouldn't have had the money in the desk. That I know. But still the matter has to be taken care of.

DISCUSSION

At one time or another, administrators can expect to be informed by teachers or children that forbidden objects have been brought by some children to school, or that property has been stolen. Various techniques for handling such situations have been used. How far school staffs go in the actual physical search of children to uncover suspected infractions of the rules is highly significant. Relationship to the dominant-subordinate relation between children and adults and respect for the personal dignity of children are both involved.

The intellect of the child, tested and recorded, is not the only part of him which is subject to surveillance by the school. In addition, both his physical person and his property are considered within the rights of inspection by school authorities. In the case of the physical person, parents may be asked to give permission for medical examinations, but apparently cursory matters such as inspection of hair, skin, eyes, and ears are frequently conducted without such permission. The rights of the person, however, are generally respected in that more intimate medical examination is ordinarily not undertaken without regard for the legal rights of parents and guardians. This is in good measure because the medical profession itself has worked out techniques for guarding itself against legal involvements. Thus, permission slips for examinations and inoculations must be signed by parents, and female teachers are usually assigned to be present when male physicians examine girls.

Less consideration is extended to the matter of examining personal property of children. This occurs for reasons that school people generally attribute to safety considerations within schools. However, it involves rather serious implications for the relationship between students and teachers, school and community, and among children themselves. Schools often have unwritten rules concerning those possessions which children are permitted to bring to school and those subject to confiscation. In the anecdotes presented here the teachers are uncertain how to handle the matter of cigarettes in the classroom or stolen property. They look to the assistant principal and principal for direction. The first teacher's initial sentiment is that of respect for the child's right to his package of cigarettes so long as it does not interfere with the classroom (it is the infringement of the rule of walking to the basket before three o'clock that disturbs her). The matter of the cigarettes is a relatively minor one, however, for the range of objects that enter the school includes far more potentially serious things, e.g., knives or other weapons.

In schools where some pupils are suspected of bringing dangerous, frightening, or forbidden objects to school, or where stealing occurs, the decisions of the administration on how to handle the matter have important implications for the relations between the children and the staff, the school and community. How to handle these situations varies from the private, discreet conference with child, parents, or guardians,

Who Stole the Cookie Money?

with possible professional resolution of the youngster's problem, to the public shakedown and the undignified frisking of the child.

SHAKEDOWNS AND FRISKING Shakedowns and frisking are names of two techniques employed by school staff when searching children. These methods are utilized when the school administration suspects that gang or personal fights are planned, and that weapons, or other forbidden objects, have been brought into the school building. Search may also be initiated as a result of robbery within the building, as, for example, when money is missing from a teacher's purse. In the case of anticipated violence, a pupil may alert a teacher, dean, guidance counselor, or assistant principal. Teachers or other staff members may have overheard plans or discussion by pupils. Generally, the news is relayed to the principal, who is the one who gives permission for the search to take place.

While the shakedown and frisking are both methods of search, in this discussion there is a basic difference between the two. The shakedown is conducted publicly, in the classroom. Frisking, on the other hand, is conducted privately, for example, in the dean's office or in the lavatory, and involves a physical search of clothing and body.[1]

In the case of the shakedown, a male member of the administration, with some reputation as an authority figure, will enter a classroom, ask that the class stand and empty all pockets and purses onto the desks. There is some physical contact in the form of tapping and poking at the pockets of the children. Boys' trousers are sometimes rolled up in order to see if weapons are concealed in socks or on the leg. The items displayed are then perused for potential weapons, stolen or forbidden property. Among the items confiscated are knives, bottle openers, bits of antennas, garrison belts, buckles. Cigarettes, prophylactics, model airplane glue, and carbona are sometimes confiscated as well.

---

[1] The matter of the shakedown and frisking that takes place in schools is highly significant. Yet practically nothing is written on this subject. The description of these occurrences in urban schools reported here comes from the author's personally conducted observation and interviews.

Where individuals are suspected of carrying weapons not uncovered by the shakedown, they are subjected to a frisking. Very often, in these cases, the police are called in to do the actual searching. Boys are generally searched in an office; girls by a female teacher in the lavatory.

Those school people who engage in shakedowns and frisking insist that these procedures are essential to ensure the safety of the pupils in situations where violence is anticipated. They do not think in terms of violating the privacy of the person or persons being searched. They consider the activity an act of prevention. However, the effects are potentially negative as well.

The reactions of the children vary. Those with no involvement in conflict with authority and no history of anti-social behavior become very excited by the shakedown. The experience tends to deepen their fear of youngsters outside of their own social group. There tends to be exaggeration concerning the nature of the danger to themselves and their friends, home, and community, for they are rarely told why the search is being conducted.

In situations where the youngsters are familiar with the patterns of anti-authoritarian behavior, the pupils frequently agitate and provoke the searchers. The teacher is egged on. For example, "You forgot to look here, teach!"

There is a great deal of hooting at the person who is caught. Such a child suffers genuine humiliation in the eyes of his peers. The one who has brought weapons to school and is not caught, on the other hand, derives increased prestige among his fellows for having outwitted the school authorities. Bragging ensues, for having been able to instigate the shakedown or frisking and not be caught represents a victory to be celebrated.

As already stated, those who engage in shakedowns and frisking rationalize this activity as ensuring the safety of pupils, which is regarded as more important than the personal privacy and dignity of the individual. That some staff people enjoy this practice as a means of establishing authority is also true, for this is a battle between the pupils and those who wish to exert a dominance over youngsters whom they basically distrust, fear, and wish to maintain in a subordinate role. Some-

Who Stole the Cookie Money?

times, frisking occurs even without overt provocation. As one dean stated, "Sometimes I frisk a kid to annoy him—just to let him know that if he wants me to stay off his back I want him to keep things out of school."

It has already been described how the shakedown humiliates some, frightens others, and serves to increase social distance between different elements in the school population, and enhances the prestige of others who are not "caught." Frisking is potentially also an extremely degrading experience to the child. For one, if he should be found to have weapons, he has been "caught." In cases where personal property is confiscated, as sometimes happens with cigarettes, there is great anger and resentment. For some children, considerable financial investment is involved. Also, many argue that their parents have given them permission to smoke. For the innocent, it is a painful reminder of their subservient position in school and the presence of inappropriate demeanor on the part of the authorities that conveys to children the indignity of their subservient position as pupils.

In addition to the personal destruction involved in these experiences for children, the procedures can reinforce hatred of the police. They also serve to destroy rapport with any staff member who is suspected of betraying the confidence of the child. The professionally trained, licensed guidance counselor shies away from direct involvement in shakedowns and frisking. Generally, the administrative staff, particularly the assistant principals and the dean within the school, are the most directly involved.

It is extremely difficult to document the frequency of this activity in schools, although it appears that the frequency is greatest in schools with the heaviest concentration of lower-class, minority group children, where suspicion and mistrust of the pupils is greatest. Schools that are predominantly white and middle class almost never have shakedowns. Infractions of rules in these schools are handled discreetly, privately, and with greater respect for person and public reputation. Schools with integrated populations may have one or two shakedowns a year. One school, on the other hand, with a high percentage of minority group pupils defined as behavior problems, routinely searches its student body every morning at nine and every afternoon at three, with strict rules concerning what the contents of the pockets may be, including the amount of money carried.

Shakedowns and frisking, then, are basically techniques to reinforce the subordinate role of pupils in the school. While they appear to offer a way of preventing trouble, they have developed in some instances into a continuous challenge between youngsters who have little other way of hitting back at what they regard as repressive authority, and schools which seek to maintain the traditional power relationship. In a heterogeneous school situation, i.e., racially mixed or socially mixed, they serve to strengthen the fears of danger which act to prevent communication essential for constructive integration. Administrators who engage in this behavior toward one segment of the school population and not the other in such mixed schools can be accused of prejudice by the community and the children.

Thus, for example, in a recent incident a principal who searched black girls and not the white girls in a newly integrated school incurred the wrath of those concerned with the treatment of black youngsters by the white staffs of the schools they were now attending.

Whether shakedowns and frisking aid as a safety measure or whether they increase the potential for friction is a question worth asking. The important subject of frisking is not ordinarily discussed in training courses for school supervisors or teachers, but it should be.

CHAPTER 13

Parents

> The school removes the child from the private world of the family and prepares him for the public world of work. The absence of parents from school does not necessarily indicate lack of concern or disinterest in the education of their children. Rather, a complex set of factors is involved.
>
> **Mrs. Bender**
> **Grade 5/2**

November 9. I have lunch sometimes with fifteen to twenty teachers who all eat there, in the little tearoom in the assistant principal's office. It gets very crowded. As far as discussions go, some of the women who had gone to Europe with their husbands were discussing Europe this week. They were talking about the trips to Europe for the summer and most of them were discussing holidays and vacations. One teacher was discussing the principal. She had put on a beautiful, beautiful play at Election Day with her class. The play was written by the children themselves and after the play was given to the fifth- and sixth-grade assembly, the principal, who had observed the play at this particular assembly, questioned the children as to who liked the play, as if to imply that the children really didn't like it. The children backed the teacher up. The children had written the play and they told him so.

Also, before he praised them about the beautiful job the

children had done, he yelled at them and he said he only saw two parents there. "Why aren't there more parents here?" He said it was a terrible showing.

The kids had worked so hard for this play. They had written it themselves and they acted it out beautifully, but he started yelling at them because the parents weren't there. Then he asked one girl why her parents weren't there and she said her parents work. This sort of held him back because he stopped asking them why individual parents were not there, but the teacher was very upset. She felt that he should not have said anything of this sort about parents not being there. He should have said that parents are invited, and that's it. He had already known that parents were invited to come. It was unfortunate that only two turned up. But she was just fuming and said that he had no right to do what he did.

November 16. This week was Open School Week. Parents visited the school on Thursday morning. Four parents showed up in my class. They started coming in at ten in the morning. They observed the reading lesson and then we moved on to our regular seats and we started social studies oral reports.

One of the girls, Roberta, gave her oral report and then William gave his. I noticed that the reports started serious oral discussion. Children whose parents were not there wanted to be recognized to answer questions—to do extra things. They wanted recognition. That was the entire thing. It is obvious to me at this point that these children definitely lack love and affection and I only wish I were able to divide myself into so many people and to just work with each one individually and give him the attention that he needs. As far as the children whose parents were there were concerned, they, of course, were interested in showing their parents exactly what they do in school and of course those are the children who are actually my good children, the ones who very rarely give me any problems.

Linda's mother came. Linda is the best student in the class. She is alert, awake, and to top it all off she is very quiet and very, very understanding—very perceptive. Her mother was there with her aunt. Pedro's mother was there. Juan's father was there and that was it as far as parents were concerned.

It was just four parents and I was very, very upset after the parents left, realizing that all of these children are actually lacking love and attention and that they put on a good show, so to speak, only because there were parents in the room and they resented the fact that it was not their parent who was there to see what was going on in the school.

**Miss Seabold
Grade 1/5**

November 16. I learned from the experienced teachers that usually they (the parents) don't come until the evenings, and, of course, those parents that you'd like to see most never come, and those that you don't really have to speak with, come.

DISCUSSION

One of the characteristic complaints made by the staff members of urban slum schools concerns their difficulty in engaging the parents of the children. Teachers and administrators often speak of lack of co-operation and the relative lack of involvement of the urban poor parent in the formal education of his child. Open School Week in such schools have tended to draw relatively low attendance compared to the high attendance in more affluent neighborhoods, and, as the teachers here have stated, this is frequently interpreted to indicate the parent's lack of involvement in the education of his child. In addition, emotional deprivation, the absence of love and affection, is inferred. Many of the comments made about slum school parents ignore the social reality surrounding parent-school relations and are also permeated with distortions concerning parental attitudes.

Parent-school relations cannot be adequately understood without reference to the fact that the school in contemporary metropolitan society has socializing functions for children that are not always congruent with those of the family. The school as an institution plays the role of removing the child from the private world of the family and prepares him for the public world of work. Prior to the development of a highly industrialized, urban society, on the farm and in the small town the life of the family and the world of work were more closely related. In our time:

> *There is the private world of family and friends, of domestic life and sociability, of home and its environs. Its harmonies and tensions are rooted in values and expressed in emotions which are quite separate from the other, outer and sometimes even hostile world of the great social superstructures. These latter—the corporately organized activities of industry, agriculture, finance, business, transportation, government, education, religion, and health—constitute the public world, which stands counterpoised structurally and spatially apart, in the great social and cultural dichotomy which characterizes our civilization.*[1]

That the school functions to prepare the child for his place in the public world of the corporate society is true for the children of all social and economic classes. Concern for the progress of their children in school is expected of middle-class parents. Parental pressures to ensure successful achievement are exerted. Some slum school teachers and administrators have been known to express preference for working in lower-class neighborhoods in order to avoid the surveillance of middle-class parents,[2] whose anxiety that their children move successfully into the higher-status positions in the corporate world creates pressures on both the children and the school.

Concern for their children is not limited to the middle and upper classes, and an upsurge in community pressures upon schools in the inner city has been taking place. What is sometimes distinctive about the slum school is the way in

---

[1] Solon Kimball and James E. McClellan, *Education and the New America*, New York: Random House, 1962, p. 35.

[2] Howard S. Becker, "The Career of the Chicago Public School Teacher," *American Journal of Sociology*, Vol. 57, 1932, pp. 470–77.

which parental concern is expressed and the way in which it is regarded by the school.

Ordinarily the inner-city school presents real barriers to the poor while at the same time protesting its wish for parent involvement. The most obvious barriers are physical, i.e., locked doors, guards, and the requirement for entry permits. While these are designed for the protection of the children, they also act as physical barriers to parents during the time their children are under surveillance by the school. This separation exists for middle-class parents as well, though not in the same degree. More important than the physical, however, are the social barriers between the slum school and the parent, which make engagement between parents and the personnel of the school difficult.[3]

The first and most obvious social barrier is that the staff and administration of the school invariably live outside the area in which it exists, and move in a private world very different from that of the parents. Thus, choice of car, trip to Europe, clothing, careers of their children, etc., are frequent topics of conversation. The relationship with the pupils is temporary and ends with the school day. There is little visiting in homes except by especially designated personnel, such as attendance officers who check on absence and return truants to the physical plant of the school. Frequently, fear and discouragement on the part of the school authorities contributes to the rapid dissipation out of the neighborhood on the part of the school staff. Parents and neighborhood groups are made clearly aware of the incursive nature of the school institution and their subservient relationship to it.

Another aspect of the social boundaries that exist between the school and the poor is related to the use of formal language. Profanity, ungrammatical speech, street language, idiomatic speech, and dialect variations of English, as well as the use of a foreign language, are seriously frowned upon. These requirements for formal language have obvious educational aims and most educators would argue that it is the duty or function of the school to teach formal language to enable children to take their place in the larger society. There

[3] Elizabeth Eddy, *Walk the White Line,* New York: Doubleday Anchor Books, 1967.

is no argument with this goal. However, not only does this have serious implications with regard to communication with children, but also the use of formal language is inhibiting to the slum school parent who sometimes lacks the poise and knowledgeability to communicate comfortably with the school personnel. This can lead to avoidance of being present or talking to the teacher. It makes the parent painfully aware that he does not have the skills his child needs to do well in school, and, accordingly, he leaves the job to the school.

The use of formal language and the intricacies of the bureaucratic organization interfere with parent-teacher communication in still other ways. Thus, for example, pupil performance on national standardized tests for many years, in many places, was kept from them, the excuse being that the parents do not understand such complex matters as percentiles, raw scores, etc. This could lend itself to explosive situations when parents find that their children are unqualified for academic programs and even for graduation.

Also, slum parents have little control over the staffing and curriculum of the schools in their areas. While this is also true of more affluent groups in metropolitan areas, they, if dissatisfied with the personnel or performance of the school, are in a better position to exercise the options of movement to school systems more compatible with their interests, or transfer into private schools. In addition, the fact that fewer social boundaries exist between the parents of middle-class areas and the personnel of the school enables them to exercise a greater measure of control over the education of their children through the use of such mechanisms as tutoring, discussions with teachers, or activity in formally recognized groups such as parents' associations which operate in socially acceptable ways.

Yet the slum schools do make an effort, often begrudgingly, to engage parents in a school-home partnership, often with limited success, as the Open School Week description here indicates. To dismiss this as a result of parental indifference or to view it as lack of love and affection for the children represents a gross oversimplification of the problem. Parental love and affection and interest cannot be measured by the attendance of the parent in school. Obviously, parents do not come to school for a variety of reasons. Some of these reasons grow out of the social barriers mentioned above. Others grow out of work schedules which make it difficult for the parent to come to school when asked. The principal described here was chastened by a child's comment that his parent couldn't come because of work. The teacher herself, although critical of the principal, reacted in the same manner as he to the poor attendance in her class during Open School Week. Commitment to family responsibilities or even fear of school growing out of personal experience are also involved. The feeling that they are not really welcome except to hear criticism of their children also exists.

Because parents do not come to school does not necessarily mean that they are disinterested or even alienated. It may, on the contrary, indicate that the parent is quite satisfied with the work of the school. It may even indicate that the parent has complete trust in the school's handling of the children.[4] The school and the teacher are often viewed by those who are unfamiliar with the bureaucracy, or those who are without power in the corporate world, as being responsible for the preparation of the children. For the poor of relatively recent rural backgrounds, and for populations with little formal education, the school is viewed as having the function of educating the child for the technologically oriented corporate society. Rural backgrounds, minimal schooling, and unskilled occupations have made the parents dependent upon the public institution of the urban school to educate the children for the new lives they will have to lead if they are to be integrated into the society. It is unrealistic for the school to define parental dependence and trust in the school to educate and care for children as irresponsibility on the part of the parents, for those living in extreme poverty and those who have not been incorporated into the public world often lack the knowledgeability to help their children make this transition.

The middle-class parent often appears more co-operative with the school because he is equipped with the skills to enable his child to move successfully through the grades, and the

[4] Elena Padilla, *Up from Puerto Rico*, New York: Columbia University Press, 1958, p. 206.

schools seem to be functioning to enable his children to take their place among higher-status positions of the corporate society. More often than not, the lower-class parent also regards the school as functioning adequately. Only as the massive educational failure of inner-city school populations has driven home the realization that the possibilities for vertical mobility through educational achievement are limiting the life chances of their children have more militant confrontations taken place between the inner-city schools and parents, usually in the form of school boycotts, sometimes in the form of individual parents confronting teachers and/or administrators, often in ways not socially acceptable to the school.[5]

These activities represent genuine concern for the children's life chances based on a recognition that increasingly American society demands school success and certification for entry into competition for the higher social status positions and escape from poverty. Thus, massive educational failure of inner-city schools has led to parental protest, in itself a real though unpopular and even socially unacceptable form of engagement—more recently, in demand for local control over schools.

Often, when parents are asked to the slum school, it is on the school's terms and the parental role is clearly subservient to that of the school. Thus, the parent is asked to come when his child is in trouble and often he does not. "The ones that you'd like to see most never come, and those that you don't really have to speak with, come" is a common reflection of this. Again, those parents who do not appear at school when their children are in academic or behavioral difficulty stay away for many different reasons. It must be emphasized that most parents do come if summoned. The absence of a parent may indicate illness, work, fear, embarrassment, and even helplessness in not being able to control the influence of peers, mass media, urbanization, and other social forces as they have created a child and a world over which the parent has no control. It can, of course, reflect neglect, disinterest, or alienation of some from the organized social order of which the school represents a major institution. In any huge popu-

[5] Estelle Fuchs, *Pickets at the Gates,* New York: The Free Press (Macmillan), 1966.

lation, problems of mental deficiency, pathology, or irresponsibility apply to some. In such instances it is cruel to the child for the school to penalize him or embarrass him for the shyness or deficiency of the parent. Confrontation with the school on these terms can lead to deteriorating parent-child relations or hostility toward the school. Sometimes a parent's avoidance of school can reflect emotional support for the child who has confronted a hostile school environment.

Slum schools are not without efforts to please parents. Plays, musical programs, food festivals, etc. are often held. When parents do not attend these events in large numbers, teachers and administrators are very disappointed, and since they have made parental attendance a goal, the children are likely to be disappointed as well. It is curious that a school system which does not teach by entertainment does nonetheless seek to entertain parents and other visitors. Parents are invited, again on the school's terms, to see a show or witness a special lesson. On display this way, the teacher and the class respond with very entertaining and interesting programs. All of these activities can be very nice and pleasant. They represent very worth-while ways of incorporating children into school activities and exposing them to the content of the larger culture. A dramatic representation of Election Day, for example, has great educational potential. As efforts to engage parents they have limited value. Their public relations aspect does not always make up for academic failure or the physical and social barriers that exist between the schools and the poor, and more often than not the parent is concerned with *his* child's progress, not group performances.

The lower-class and minority group populations confined to the inner city are dependent upon the public schools to prepare their children to move from the private world of the family to the public world of work. Some parents are far more consciously aware than others of the significance of this transition and are making demands upon the schools, ranging from the right to take a reader home to help a child to demands for control over curriculum, staffing, and expenditure of school funds. Others are not so committed to formal education and the schools must assume the responsibility for preparing the child for the public world.

Efforts to engage parents, if they persist in keeping the parent subservient, entertaining him, or summoning him and berating him because his child is more of a problem than others, are not likely to develop good parent-school relations. More often than not, the parent would like to co-operate and does not have the skill. Honest reporting to parents and respect for their concern are essential. Removing the physical and social barriers separating school and parent would contribute to genuine engagement of parents with the school, if this be the aim. While the barriers exist and the parents are viewed as low men in a hierarchical arrangement, home-school partnership in the slum school will continue to remain unsatisfactory.

PART IV

ADJUSTING

CHAPTER 14

The Observation: A *Rite de Passage*

> The granting of a license and the assignment of a teaching position are not by themselves adequate to make the teacher feel she has been incorporated into the status of teacher. She remains in the highly dangerous period of transition, during which time she has not fully internalized the feelings of full membership which bring with them commitment to the status, nor is she as yet being treated by the institution as one who belongs as a fully responsible teacher. In order for her to complete the transition, provision has to be made for the teacher to be claimed by the school. Rituals, such as the observation, can help to perform this function.

Miss Winters
Grade 2/4

November 2. The most important thing that happened to me in my school this week was that I was told that I was going to be observed next Thursday. This was to be a formal observation. I was expected to give a reading lesson. That is what my assistant principal told me. She gave me a form on which I was to fill out the basic outline of my lesson and I submitted that to her on Friday and she was going to go over it and give it back to me on Monday. If there's anything in it that she sees that she doesn't like she will let me know.

She told me that the purpose of this observation is not to trick us or to see what we do wrong or right or any reason like that. The purpose of this observation is to see how we react in a teaching situation. She knows that there will be many good things that we will do and many bad things that we will do. Likewise we should not feel at all hurt or in any way unhappy when she criticizes the lesson. The assistant principal is going to be taking notes in shorthand and she told us she will be writing all the time.

I think that this was the most important thing that happened to me. Because I had been wondering when I was going to be observed, and I kept saying to myself, "Maybe they will never come. Why aren't they coming?" But now I know they are coming Thursday and I know exactly what is expected of me. They want to see reading, and I know exactly what they are going to be looking for. She's going to follow the guide for that lesson and I know that it should be all right. I am not nervous about it because, as I said before, no matter who would come in, I would give the same kind of lesson, but this time I know exactly what is expected of me so I will be able to do it a little bit better. Of course, yesterday we got paid again. But that isn't the most important thing that happened, but it was important.

November 9. The most important thing that happened to me in my school this week was that I had my first formal observation. My feeling when this took place was that I was very nervous. Prior to the lesson I had a gym period. I was extremely nervous in this gym period. My stomach was jumping because, actually, although I said I wouldn't be nervous when the time came, I was very nervous. However, when we left the gym and were going into the classroom I said to myself, "Gee, if I get nervous I'll ruin the lesson altogether, so I've got to try to just pretend they're not in the room." That's exactly what I did. Mr. Trent, that's my principal, and Mrs. Parker, the assistant principal, came. When they came in I started the lesson.

The first thing that I did was to have the books passed out

The Observation: A Rite de Passage

and then I started my lesson. The lesson was a reading lesson from the basal reader, *Fun with Dick and Jane*. I did a story, "Funny, Funny Sally," and that story was Sally was in the kitchen helping Mother and Sally had frosting on her cake—Sally had frosting of the cake on her face and she did not know it and that's why everybody said she was funny.

The motivation for the lesson was "Did you ever help your mother?" Then I got from the children the ways in which they help their mothers, until one child said that he helped his mother beat up the batter for a cake. When I got that I said, "Oh, that's wonderful! Today we're going to see how Sally helped her mother and later on you will help me bake a cake."

The children liked that idea. Then we went over the reading. I had them look over the page and then I had them tell me who was talking and what they said—not read it but tell me. When that was done I had them pretend that they were Grandma or Sally or Jane. Then they read what was said.

After we finished the story in that manner, I got the utilities for making the cake. I had the bowl, the egg beater, instant frosting, and hot water. We put the frosting in the bowl and beat it up. The children came and stood around and watched and while the children did this I more or less acted as a participant observer.

The assistant and Mr. Trent, the principal, left at that point. They didn't wait until the cake was finished. So I finished the lesson with the children with a lot of relief and sighing because it was over.

Before the principal left he said it was a nice lesson. He liked it very much. Then Mrs. Parker arranged for a formal conference with me. At this conference she had a long list of things that she had been writing while the lesson was going on. I had seen her writing but I didn't even bother to think about what she may have been writing because I didn't want to get myself involved about what was going on. I was very nervous but not to the point where it showed. She told me she liked the lesson but there were a few things that she didn't like. These were mostly technical things that I would pick up as I went along. She said that she didn't like the idea of my going as slowly as I went. However, I thought that this criticism was a little unjustified because I felt I knew my children and I knew exactly how slowly I have to go with them. I have been doing this since September. It's the only way that I get the results. I can't rush the children. If I ask the children to read the page and tell me in their own words what the characters are saying, I must give them time. If Sally says, "This is fun," I don't want them to read for me "This is fun." I want them to tell me, "Sally said making the cake was fun," or something like that. So I give them time.

She also said that, in general, the discipline routines and the rapport were good but she would like to see a little more or a little less—I forget how she said it—but anyway, she wants to see the children doing more during the lesson but, actually, during a reading lesson I don't know what more they can do.

In general, she said she liked the lesson but she needed to criticize because I was new. But she told me that she was very well pleased with it and satisfied and that I shouldn't worry about it.

**Miss Peters
Grade 4/3**

October 26. The principal had sent around a notice saying that he would be around to observe us either at the end of this week or sometime next week. When I saw him on Thursday, he told me he would be in either that afternoon or on Friday. I was very nervous that afternoon and I was nervous all day Friday. Friday afternoon he told me that he wouldn't be in until sometime next week. I asked him if he wanted me to prepare a special formal lesson for him and he said no. He just wanted to see a normal, routine day.

I rode to college with another sixth-grade teacher after school one day and she was speaking to me about many, many things related to the curriculum. She told me what it was like when she was a new teacher and she was starting out. She told me that she was still teaching time to her class. She suggested that I request certain materials from the assistant principal and that I request some little clocks that the children can use. She also told me about a game that I could play with them. It's called Quizmo and it has to do with clocks.

The Observation: A Rite de Passage

She told me she had the game in her room and if I wanted, I could request it from her. I appreciated her advice very much.

Then she told me certain things that the principal would look for when he came in to observe me. She said, for example, that he likes the teacher to call on children to evaluate each other's answers. For example, if I were to call on Stuart and he would answer, I should call on another one and ask that girl what she thought of Stuart's answer. She also told me that the principal likes to take over in the middle of the lesson. And she told me that he really didn't know very much about reading, so it really didn't pay to do a reading lesson, but that he likes to see social studies, and he also likes to see some routines. I also appreciated this very much and told her so.

November 9. The most important thing that happened to me in my school this week was that I was observed by the principal on Monday morning. I will describe to you exactly what happened to me on Monday morning. We had just finished taking the attendance and having current events when the principal walked in with another girl and he said to me, "I would like this girl to observe a new teacher. If you don't mind, could she please stay in your class for a while?"

"Fine," I said. "Of course."

Then he told me that he would be back in five minutes to observe me and he asked me what I was going to teach.

"What I usually do Monday mornings, reading, or," I told him, "I could do spelling."

He said that he wanted me to do a reading lesson, so when he left I had to get ready.

I couldn't really prepare my class in advance because there had been another class in the room earlier. Also, when the children have reading, they change seats and group one sits on one side of the room and group two sits on the other. I had just arranged the room in a different order—the order of a horseshoe, which is much more informal—and the children weren't prepared. They didn't know which seats to take and so this was really, in short, a bad time that he picked to ob-

DONALD E. GREENE

serve me. Well, I had only five minutes to get the children in their seats. They, of course, were wonderful and wonderful throughout the whole lesson. They changed into their seats as quickly and quietly as they could and then I began the reading lesson. Shortly after the principal walked in with another lady. Now there were three people observing me!

I went about my reading lesson as I ordinarily do and this is really my weakest point. This is the weakest curriculum area for me because as a new teacher it is very difficult to work with two groups because while you're working with one group, the other one has to be kept busy and vice versa. You have to motivate two groups and you have to teach two groups and it is difficult. It's proving to be easier and easier for me, but I was sorry that he picked this particular time to come in and observe me.

Another reason that I was sorry to be observed in reading was that I'd been told not to give a reading lesson for the principal because "he doesn't know anything about reading." It seems that one of the assistant principals is in charge of reading and the principal is in charge of social studies and science and math and all the other areas.

Well, I taught the reading. I have been taking a reading course on Wednesday afternoons and this has proven to be very helpful to me. I do use many of the suggestions which they give us in this course. Before the principal walked out of the room, he said to me that he enjoyed the lesson very much and that he found the lesson to be very good. He said that there were a few more points that he wanted to tell me and then the lesson would be perfect. When he left, I complimented the class on its behavior.

When I went downstairs for lunch the principal came over to me and he took up most of my lunch hour telling me about the observation. He criticized me on two things. Number one, the way that I teach the words—which is by teaching both groups' words to the whole class. This is what I've been told to do in the reading course and this was what the assistant principal told me to do and this is what I myself have found very effective. He criticized this, and the other thing he criticized is one of the drill games which I use and which I have also learned from this course. In short, the only things that

The Observation: A Rite de Passage

he criticized me for were things that the assistant principal had told me to do and things which I had gotten from the reading course.

He told me that I had excellent control over the class—an excellent manner with the children—he said I had established a very good relationship with the class and myself, he said the teaching was effective because I stressed "Does it make sense?" and I also taught the words very carefully, using illustrations. He said that the room was very neat, he liked the bulletin boards. He complimented me on many, many areas. As I said before, his only criticisms were in the two areas where I had been instructed to teach this way.

Well, of course, I felt good that he had complimented me on these other several areas, but at the same time it was bothering me that he had criticized me on those things that I had been instructed to do. Then it seems that the assistant principal and the reading teacher, who are both in charge of the reading program of this reading course, heard about the observation and this whole week there has just been a feud between them and the principal. It seems that the assistant principal is telling the principal that he is supposed to keep his hands off the reading program because she is in charge of it and then he goes ahead and criticizes one of the teachers for doing what she told her to do. I haven't yet received my observation report because the assistant principal told the secretary not to type up anything that criticizes what I did in reading. It was so upsetting to me to hear this because they're really making a very big thing out of it, but now I just find that the whole thing is just rather amusing and I wish that they would get it settled among themselves—just what they would like their teachers to do.

Miss Samson
Grade 4/2

October 19. I think the most important thing that happened to me this week was the observation of my lesson by Mr. Reid. He also brought with him Mrs. Crawford, the science co-ordinator. She passed the test for assistant principal so he said she needed practice in observations, and he brought with him a boy who has been subbing in our school, a new teacher, whom they feel they can offer a permanent position shortly. He has no student teaching credits, so he later told me, and they wanted him to see the lesson.

Actually the lesson was planned. Mr. Reid was supposed to come in for a formal observation of my class, and the lesson was scheduled for ten o'clock and at 9:30 he walked in and asked me if I would mind if he brought people with him and, I don't know, I was so nervous anyhow that it really didn't make any difference, but I think that was the most exciting thing. And I had planned a lesson around a tape recorder.

We were going to interview the children in the class and find out why their parents came to New York City and why other people come to New York City because I had sent them home to find out from their parents. We had discussed the word "interview" and the reporters on television, the whole thing, and at first I couldn't get the tape recorder to work so I was sort of a nervous wreck, but then it all got organized before he got there and I gave the lesson.

At first I was nervous and upset and then as I started to give the lesson it just seemed to go very well, so I wasn't nervous any more. I saw how nervous my students were—it was a big thing, they were being watched by Mr. Reid—and then I sort of calmed down.

I hadn't planned on telling them that he was coming in, but we were discussing the tape recorder the day before and how we were going to interview, and some of them said they didn't feel they would talk into it and they were going to say silly things. Then I said, "We really should be able to talk nicely so Mr. Reid can hear. I told Mr. Reid about the nice things you found out, what important things you found out, and he's coming to listen," and they all said, "We're not going to talk. We're embarrassed." I thought, "There goes the whole thing down the drain and it would really be an interesting thing to try with them." I was planning to let them listen to the tapes so we could carry the lesson over into language arts.

So they came in and the children were on their best behavior and they were quite nervous when he got there. In fact, when I asked first for any volunteers, I didn't get any and Mr. Reid was nice enough to volunteer first and told us where his grandparents came from, and the lesson started to roll. Everybody volunteered. This also was one of the most successful lessons during the week.

**Miss Harris
Grade 2/6**

October 19. The principal came in and looked around and listened for a few minutes. However, she didn't come in at the beginning of the lesson, and she stayed only about seven minutes, and this was the formal observation that she was giving to my lesson. I felt rather discouraged because it was a rather informal lesson, and she didn't observe it in its entirety; she did look around and take a few notes. During the lesson one of the children happened to fall off his chair, which was wonderful! We had a safety discussion about chair-tippers. We're using a display of what we call nitwits. We have a chair-tipper nitwit, a stick-in-the-mouth nitwit, someone who runs around with lollipop sticks, and what happens. So, of course, everyone immediately said, "Ohhh, chair-tipper nitwit." The principal did come up and make just one comment, "Maybe if we all had our feet flat on the floor. . . ."

Needless to say, I was quite discouraged about this observation. However, Mrs. Ryan did ask me to come into her office at three, and she thought that the lesson was quite good, which I was very surprised at, since it wasn't a lesson I had spent a great deal of time preparing for. However, her main criticism was that several of the children were fooling—which was true. Two children were writing. Several times I did stop and ask them to remove the things from their desks. However, I had discovered that since my class as a whole had been a discipline problem and since we were getting someplace with the children, if one or two children were not paying attention, I would not make an issue, particularly at the time when I had the majority of the class listening to me. I found that before when I had done this that part of the class would lose interest. I explained this to Mrs. Ryan and she said that it was true but that I should try to get everyone's interest, even if I had to go over and take the things away and put them on my desk.

Another criticism was that I tended to repeat the children's answers. This I know I do and I do try to correct it. I guess it's because some of the children tend to speak quite softly and I want to tell the rest of the class. I feel that if they didn't hear the child at least by hearing me they'll know something. But of course I do agree that this isn't the best thing to do—the children should develop their own listening powers, to listen to the child and not expect to have it said to them again by the teacher.

And then the third criticism was that I tend at times to ask a child about a question before I state the question, such as, "Jerry, do you think you can tell me . . ." and then give the question. Mrs. Ryan felt that this makes the rest of the class lose interest, because they know they're not being called on. I do not agree and this one criticism I did feel I had to speak to her about. The fact is that I do not always do this. At times, however, when children are discipline problems in the class and they're not paying attention, rather than take the time to go over and stop the lesson and reprimand the child, I'd rather get his interest by saying, "Jerry," and he will drop what he is doing and look at me. I try not to do this too often, but to me this has been a very useful means of getting the children who are not paying attention without disrupting the lesson and losing the rest of the class.

She was, however, pleased with the classroom layout, the bulletin boards, the plants around the room, just the physical setup; and she felt that the children were almost aggressively interested in the lesson. The fact that we have to work on not waving hands—I agree, this has to be done—but the fact is that the children are starting to get interested in what we are doing. The fact that they're listening, almost flying out of their seats at times to answer questions, is really, I feel, quite an improvement. She agreed with this and said, "Well, just kind of try to channel it so that it's a little more organized and disciplined when the children do want to give answers." But she was quite pleased that the children are interested in the work and most of the children do pay attention. . . .

The Observation: A Rite de Passage

October 26. The most important thing that happened to me in school this week concerns two letters which I received from the principal and assistant principal. These were in reference to visits made by these supervisors and their observations of my classroom, the children, and the subject matter which was being taught at the time they came into the room. Mrs. Ryan, the principal, had visited my class a week ago Friday for her observation and I had to speak to her Friday afternoon concerning the visit. However, this week I received my formal letter from her. A copy of this letter, I believe, is sent to the district supervisor, another is kept in the school, another is given to me, and I'm not sure where the last copy goes.

Mrs. Ryan's letter was very brief. The first line was very encouraging. It said that she had noticed a great deal of improvement in the children, especially in the discipline of the children. The remainder of the letter contained several suggestions. One, of course, was the one I mentioned last week that she had told me during our conference—I should never call on a person before I pose the question. I already explained why I did this—the idea of getting a child who is not interested and who is fooling around to listen to what I was saying. This was something I did all the time.

The second criticism, however, I felt was a useful one. She said that I must remember not to repeat the children's answers, and I know that this is a fault of mine and I've been trying to work on it this week.

The third was, of course, to see that all the children are sitting up tall and straight with their feet flat on the floor so that there's no wriggling around or tipping of chairs. This was about the complete letter that Mrs. Ryan sent.

**Miss Peters
Grade 4/3**

December 7. During the past three weeks several very important things happened to me in my school. The first thing happened about four weeks ago when the teachers of the school did a very wonderful thing which surprised and delighted me very much. It seems that they had all gotten together and had decided to take my girl friend and myself out for lunch that Tuesday, I believe it was November 19, and the reason they were going to take us out to lunch was because we had both gotten engaged. This was going to be a form of celebration. Tuesday, the nineteenth, in the afternoon was the parents' conference day, so we could have an extension at lunch period. They brought a notice around to all the teachers to have it signed concerning what food they wanted to order. And the boy by mistake brought the notice to my room so I wasn't really surprised. However, the thought really touched me and that Tuesday we all went to an Italian restaurant and the girls had chipped in and they had bought us corsages. The corsages were white orchids and they were just beautiful and the whole thing was such a lovely thought and a lovely gesture. I really felt very warm inside and I was quite happy.

DISCUSSION

Characteristic of all human life is its dynamic quality. Individuals are born, mature, and die. They respond to changes in season and climate. In addition, because men live in societies, they must make adjustments to the various positions in the social order which they hold in their lifetime. These adjustments are neither accidental nor are they anarchical in nature, for all cultures provide for a structuring of those periods of transition through which an individual or group must pass in order to provide for an orderly procession through the life cycle.

The study of cultures indicates that, despite the universality of structuring, those events which the culture chooses to emphasize as marking the transition from one status to another vary widely. Also, the same kind of event can be treated differently. For example, although physiological considerations may set limits, the time at which an individual is considered to be born can vary, and where the culture practices rites of initiation to indicate that the new individual is a member of the society, the timing of these rites differs a great deal. Social death, too, is a different phenomenon than physiological death, and is marked at different times and in different ways by various cultures.

Man's response to season and climate is also in large measure determined by the culture practiced by his group. Thus, for example, agricultural peoples are more likely to mark those changes relevant to planting and harvesting than are hunting peoples.

Associated with these culturally defined periods of movement from one state of social functioning to another have been the ceremonials or rituals which help to mark the period of change. These ceremonials have vastly enriched the content of mankind's emotional, artistic, and creative life. They tend to be traditional in content, and range from the joyous to solemn in mood. They are events to be remembered, for their significance is great and they provide the punctuation marks, as it were, to the major periods of one's lifetime.

The French anthropologist Arnold van Gennep studied ritual behavior as it affected individual life crisis, and his findings contribute immeasurably to an understanding of ritual and its relation to the dynamics of individual and group life.[1] Van Gennep termed these ceremonies *rites de passage,* i.e., rites of passage. Basically, he described a schema or structure through which an individual had to pass while moving from one social status position to another. His schema consisted of three parts. One is separation, the other transition, and the third incorporation. What this means is that ceremonials that enable individuals to move from one status to another generally include a separation out from another or former status, a period of transition, and a period of incorporation into the new status, the incorporation requiring that the individual be claimed by others in the new status. An obvious example of this is the marriage ceremony familiar to us—the father or some substitute *gives* the bride away, she remains in transition until the groom says, "I take this woman . . . ," and she is claimed as a bride, or married woman.

---

[1] Arnold van Gennep, *The Rites of Passage,* Chicago: The University of Chicago Press, 1960. Van Gennep's theory is also discussed in Eliot D. Chapple and Carleton S. Coon, *Principles of Anthropology,* New York: Henry Holt & Company, 1942, pp. 484–506.

Of course, perfunctory ceremonials by themselves do not perform the functions of movement into new statuses. *Rites de passage* mark a whole new series of relationships among people, and the father who refuses to regard his daughter as the wife of another or the husband who continues to behave as if unmarried create serious problems for the young woman involved. Nonetheless, the ceremonial provides the social recognition that a new relationship does now exist, and thus the individual involved has the social recognition that he or she is in a new status.

Ceremonials surrounding birth, puberty, marriage, and death may appear to be a far cry from the problems faced by young, new teachers in modern urban school situations. But the fact remains that even in our highly complex, secularized, urban society, individuals and those in relation to them are confronted with the problems of adjustment involved in the movement from one social status to another, and the absence of rituals to ensure the success of movement from one status to another may have profound implications for our understanding of the personal conflicts and the needs of people in our society. The implications for our society have been suggested by Solon Kimball, who writes:

> *The continued expansion of an industrial-urban civilization has produced extensive changes in our social system. Prominent among these have been increased secularization and the decline in the importance of sacred ceremonialism. Rites of passage were often, but not necessarily, tied to supernatural sanctions and to the activity of priestly intermediaries. . . . There is no evidence that a secularized urban world has lessened the need for ritualized expression of an individual's transition from one status to another. . . .*[2]

Professor Kimball makes the point that individuals who are not successfully separated and successfully incorporated are in a dangerous position. To remain in a state of transition without being claimed into the new status leaves the indi-

[2] In Arnold van Gennep, op. cit., pp. 16–17.

The Observation: A Rite de Passage

vidual open to myriad problems, including that of search for identity and alienation from society.

Beginning teachers in the urban metropolis are entering into a new status. They have already been separated from teacher education institutions where they were students by having been graduated. (The very grammatical usage in the language connotes the separating out away from.) Of course, many will continue to be students, some seeking further qualifications in the field of education, others moving to new careers, some finding their school studies a form of attachment they cannot give up. From the point of view of the college, however, once a degree has been granted, there is no longer any direct responsibility for that individual as a student, preparing for a degree to enable him to be a teacher. His relationship to the institution is of another sort after graduation.

A complicating problem is that individuals occupy many status positions in society simultaneously with many different roles associated with them. The complexity of our culture is such that the young person having been separated from college and facing the problems of transition and incorporation into the status of teacher may be facing many critical life adjustments at the same time. These may create a serious drain on energies. Also, the degree of commitment possible to one or another role may be variable as a result. Thus, some are moving from the status of single to that of married, from the state of economic dependence to the state of economic independence—a factor which connotes the move into adulthood in this culture—and, most important for our considerations, from full-time student to full-time teacher.

The granting of a license and the assignment to a teaching position are not by themselves adequate to make the teacher feel she has been incorporated into the status of teacher. Although separated out from the student status, she remains in the highly dangerous period of transition during which time she has not fully internalized the feeling of full membership which brings with it commitment to the status, nor is she as yet being treated by the institution as one who belongs as a fully responsible teacher. In order for her to complete the transition, provision has to be made for the teacher to be claimed by the school.

Ritual can help to perform this function. As stated above, it is important to recognize that perfunctory ritual by itself does not accomplish this. Thus, although it is pleasant (though sometimes resented) publicly to introduce the new members of the staff to the assembled gathering of the staff at the beginning of the school year, this does not make the teacher feel that she really belongs. It does, however, serve notice to those within the institution that this person is in the process of becoming a part of it, and should be known and treated accordingly.

Other provisions for the incorporation of the teacher have to be made. Some of these are social in nature, and the acceptance of the teacher by one of the social groups within the school, at luncheons, parties, etc., helps to give her the feeling of belonging and provides ceremonial evidence to the beginner that she is an accepted member of the school community. When the beginner is given professional assignments such as membership in committees or inclusion in professional conferences, he or she is also given a sense of identification with his new position.

It would appear that the renewal of appointment and the granting of tenure mark the final claiming of the teacher. But unless these are characterized by the social and professional involvements which indicate that she is fully accepted by the staff and administration as a teacher, they may not be enough to ensure the necessary feeling of really belonging that they imply. The formal claiming of the teacher begins with the licensing and appointment to a position, and proceeds to the granting of tenure. Until finally claimed, the teacher remains in a state of transition, during which time the social insecurity of her position needs to be recognized and provided for.

The impersonal nature of large-school organization frequently means that most of the formal steps involved in becoming a member of the school, from the license through the granting of tenure, go unmarked with ceremonial. Yet every teacher, despite the lack of ritual, is aware of the emotion associated with the various notices in regard to his licensing and assignments and receiving of tenure.

There is one ritual, however, through which the majority

The Observation: A Rite de Passage

of teachers are required to pass, and which operates to provide ceremonial transition into the status of an accepted teacher. This ceremony is the first formal observation. Now, the first formal observation made by the principal or his assistant is generally not thought of as a ritual of acceptance. All supervisors learn that part of their duties includes the improvement of instruction, and they generally regard the observation as an essential element in helping the new teacher to become a more effective teacher. This the observation does in that it can affirm the teacher's acceptance within the school by the administrator; it does not necessarily help in the way that the supervisor may think.

It must be remembered that administrative authority and professional authority which helps to develop improved pedagogy on the part of the teacher are two very different things. The formal observation as it is practiced is only partially concerned with the actual improvement of teaching, although the knowledgeability of the observer may be such that the teacher does gain some helpful insights in order to improve her work. Sometimes the absence of professional authority can lead to serious confusion and difficulty, as happened in the case of the principal who criticized the teacher for doing what she had learned to do in professional courses in reading. What is more significant about the first formal observation is the ritual character of the ceremony, with its emotional content. Having successfully completed this ritual, the teacher, who often views the ceremony as an ordeal, considers herself as having passed inspection and as having received affirmation that she is truly a teacher and regarded as such by her superiors.

Some supervisors carry out the ceremony with a great deal of style, and make it highly effective in claiming the teacher by giving her a feeling of having performed satisfactorily as a teacher. Others, not recognizing its significance, or not, for one reason or another, graceful actors in the ceremonial aspects of the ritual, do a far less effective job of claiming the teacher. Their performance is so perfunctory, so clumsy, as to leave the teacher in the state of transition with its concomitant danger of her remaining unincorporated and even potentially entering the state of alienation in regard to her position. This is especially true in cases where the teachers have had unsuccessful experience with the children in their classes.

It is important to emphasize again that the professional development of the teacher does not proceed primarily from the principal's or assistant principal's formal observation. This comes, rather, from consultation and assistance from those who stand in professional rather than administrative relationship to the teacher, i.e., the specialists and other teachers. Also, professional growth from these relationships are often initiated by the teacher who seeks help and advice from these sources. Principals who are genuinely concerned for the professional improvement of staff performance would be advised to operate through these other channels, and to provide time for consultation and evaluation by the new teachers and those who stand in professional authority to them, i.e., other teachers and specialists. That the formal observation has only limited relation to professional improvement of instruction is evident from the relatively artificial atmosphere in which it takes place—the choice of subject, the timing, the presence in the class of the principal, the preparation of pupils, and the general structuring, which are all atypical of the ordinary teaching situation.

The ceremony is really very simple, although considerable time is spent by prospective supervisors learning how to conduct it, and much discussion is held concerning the significance of the variations possible in its execution. Essentially, the observation is similar from school to school, with some stylistic variations. Also, the first formal observation takes place at approximately the same time in the first semester, generally around the eighth or ninth week of teaching. The teacher is usually aware that she will be visited, although she may or may not know the specific time. In some situations the exact time of the observation is mutually agreed upon by the teacher and her supervisor. She may or may not be given a choice of subject to teach, but she usually has enough advance notice to prepare herself and the children for the event. The principal (or his assistant) arrives, and observes. He may or may not take part in the lesson; more usually he does not. Some controversy exists as to which is proper between those who feel that the supervisor should observe only and those

The Observation: A Rite de Passage

who believe he should enter into the lesson. The observer leaves at the close of the lesson or sooner—leaving sooner is often disappointing to the teacher, who is taking this very seriously. He may make a few parting comments.

Fairly soon afterward the principal conducts a conference with the teacher. Again there is variation in time and place, the purists arguing that the conference ought to take place within a few days, and in the more formal atmosphere of a conference room or principal's office. Those who engage in less formal lunchroom type conferences are viewed as behaving inappropriately. The critique and comments follow a rather consistent pattern. Some negative things and some positive things are said about the conduct of the lesson. Sometime later, these comments are presented to the teacher in the form of a letter, duplicate copies of which are sent to the appropriate files and persons.

The ceremony also includes some instruction. The teacher is generally given a structure which her lesson should follow, with emphasis upon aim and motivation. She is frequently told not to repeat the children's answers or to call on a child before asking a question. She is encouraged not to use a loud tone of voice or attempt to cover too many things in one lesson. There are, generally, comments made about the physical appearance of the room, with emphasis placed upon displaying the work of children. These instructions help remove the mystery surrounding expectation of her behavior and make it possible to face future observations with less trepidation.

During the course of the observation and subsequent conferences, the teacher has passed through an emotional crisis characterized by severe fear and nervousness, or a state of numbness. Many if not all teachers regard the observation as an ordeal through which they have to go. Having successfully passed through it, the teacher receives affirmation that she is "on the right track," that she is indeed a teacher recognized as such by her superiors.

The observation is thus a ritual through which the teacher and the principal go. The ritual affirms the teacher's incorporation into the staff, and it also affirms her subordinate position in the staff hierarchy, for it reinforces the principal's right of inspection. The ceremonial takes place at different times during the teacher's career and with decreasing frequency as the teachers have been fully incorporated into their status and have learned the behavior appropriate to it without the need for constant surveillance. It is the first observation, however, which is most critical for the beginner.

For some individuals, to be observed at any time is a difficult emotional experience, but the first observation is the most intense in its effects. Van Gennep, in his examination of *rites de passage,* found too that the degree of intensity of *rites de passage* varied. For example, second or third marriages are frequently not marked with as much ceremonial as first marriages. The first observation tends to be the most emotional experience.

The first formal observation has only limited relation to the teacher's methodology, understanding of children, and handling of curriculum content, although some instruction does take place. As stated earlier, this growth proceeds more effectively through other channels in the school, i.e., through participation in professional conferences, through contacts with specialists, other beginners, more experienced teachers, or contact with other knowledgeable persons. To exercise some control of the direction of professional growth, administrative supervisors need to be aware of these channels and can operate through them.

To really know the needs and problems of the beginning teacher requires more than sitting in the class for a brief period under conditions which are extraordinary. Observation can be of great value in helping a teacher to evaluate her functioning. However, with rare exception, under conditions of being formally observed, the teacher is acutely aware that she is being *judged*. This in itself has value if the person doing the judging leaves the teacher with the feeling that she has passed inspection, thus giving her increased confidence that her behavior is appropriate in her new status. The danger perceived by the teacher, contributing to her state of nervousness and distress, is the very real possibility that she will not be able to give appropriate evidence that she really is an acceptable teacher.

For the administrator, observing the teacher formally in this

The Observation: A Rite de Passage 163

way also confirms his position as superior to that of the teacher. At the same time, he is himself acting out administrative requirements set by those in positions superior to himself. Thus, the reports he makes, both to his superiors and to the teacher, lend themselves to perfunctory meeting of bureaucratic requirements rather than improving the quality of teaching.

CHAPTER 15

Getting Help

> Unable or unwilling to take a strong position against incompetent teachers, principals sometimes place them where it is felt the least damage to children will result. Unfortunately, this leads to a disregard for professionalism and a cynical view, for invariably the children and other teachers suffer. It also frustrates the process through which teachers get their greatest assistance.

Miss Winters
Grade 2/4

September 21. The most important thing that happened to me in school this week concerns itself with *Think and Do* books. They are workbooks that the children use in the language arts area. In this book the children are asked to underline certain words or to pick out the correct word. This exercise usually is based upon the correct following of directions and being able to make associations or word meanings.

Let me give you a specific question. There may be a picture of Sally, Dick, and Jane and the exercise may be in understanding the words *to* and *with*. Now the picture might show Sally coming with Jane. The words might say Sally comes *to* Jane, Sally comes *with* Jane, and the children are supposed to underline the correct one based on what they see in the

Getting Help

picture. I have tried to give you a little bit of an example of what is contained in the *Think and Do* books.

Now, when I gave these *Think and Do* books out, the children just wouldn't respond to it so I went to my supervisor, Miss Doyle, and I told her about this. I never expected that she would come into my classroom and give a full lesson. That is exactly what she did. She came in that very afternoon and she showed me exactly how to work with these workbooks. This really was the most important thing that happened to me this week because it really let me see exactly how to work with the children and these books. I had been doing it the first week of school and into the second week of school. This event took place on Tuesday and I wasn't having much success and I didn't know why. I thought it was the children's lack of knowledge that wouldn't allow them to do this. However, upon seeing her do this lesson I realize that it wasn't as much the children as it was that I wasn't specific enough in giving directions. I wasn't clear enough. I didn't have every one of the thirty children with me. I would just glance at a few children and when I saw that they had their eyes and fingers on the right pages I was contented with that.

However, Miss Doyle made me aware that you have to go around to each child and see that each child has it, and if there is a slow child who doesn't have it, you stay there and you work with him. I felt very happy when this happened because now I realize that this area will no longer present a problem to me, and that is why I term this the most important thing that happened in my school this week.

Miss Samson
Grade 4/2

October 12. I think the most important thing that happened to me this week was a meeting with Mr. Julian, one of the teachers on my grade, and a similar one with a few other teachers in the school. I was quite depressed this week and down in the dumps. It was personal, and I also felt that the thought of the principal coming in to watch me this week sort of set me off, because he speaks very highly of me and every time I ask him a question he tells me how well I'm going to do and what great potential I have, how well everyone else thinks I'm going to do, and here he is coming into my classroom. He says all these things and, you know, he has never really seen me teach before. I'm afraid to really think of what he's expecting. So I developed this great feeling of insecurity.

I didn't know if I was teaching correctly. Nobody had come in to see me and I resented this now. I was just on the brink of tears on Monday and Tuesday.

I had a talk with Mr. Julian. I started to complain to him about how badly I felt and everything, and he started talking to me, helping me with suggestions of what I should be teaching, what they were covering and how he was doing it, and that I shouldn't feel like that, that all new teachers feel like that and that I really can do it. I haven't got such a bad class and I'll be able to manage with them. He gave me a few tricks and short cuts. I told him what I was doing, and he was telling me what I was doing wrong. I have two groups in spelling, and he said I should eliminate that because it's a great waste of time, and both groups could do the same work. He threw a suggestion at me for social studies on different people and the reasons that they come to New York. I don't even know if it's the suggestions or just the fact that he sat and talked to me that made me feel better. I was in such a blue mood and so afraid. The fact that he might just have sat down, that somebody was helping me and caring, I think, might have set it straight and helped me a lot.

**Mrs. Bender
Grade 5/2**

December 14. The remedial reading teacher, Mr. Lee, was originally the teacher of 5/4, which is a very, very tough class. He had the children line up and he would check them or give them a cross, and he was actually what I would call a Hitler and the children listened to him. They were well disciplined, but it was to the point of abnormality. The principal, Dr. Cross (Mrs. Jones, the guidance counselor, told this to me in confidence), thought that this kind of behavior exhibited by the teacher was abnormal, and Dr. Cross felt that instead of sending him to psychiatric assistance, he would take him out of the classroom entirely, which was what was done. Mr. Lee was removed from the teaching position of 5/4 and was made an RIT, i.e., reading improvement teacher.

Now, Mr. Lee goes around to different classrooms every day. He comes to my room on Monday from ten o'clock until 10:30. We have fifteen minutes in which to prepare before he comes in. If I'm still in the room working with the children, he'll ask me, "Mrs. Bender, will you have them clear their desks?" I'm not going to fight with him, so I say, "All right," even though sometimes when I'm in the middle of a sentence, he'll walk in and say, "Mrs. Bender, please have them clear their desks."

I've spoken to him a few times about it. He just doesn't seem to comprehend. He knows that he has a time schedule. That's all he's interested in, so I tell the children to clear their desks, and while I'm preparing to take my materials out of the room, I hear what's going on: "A check for you, John, a check for you, Mary Ramon, a check for you, Felicia, very good." This is what he does. I think this is what he does the entire thirty minutes that he is in the room. He is disciplining my class.

He is just an impossible person. He's a nice person to talk to. He seems willing to help, but it's just an impossible situation when he walks out of the room and I come over to take my class back again. It is just impossible! The children breathe a heavy sigh of relief, as if to say, "Thank God he didn't do anything to me."

DISCUSSION

It does not take many days in the classroom for teachers to become cognizant of the need for help. Pressures—including lesson planning, controlling behavioral difficulties in the classroom, learning the formal administrative requirements of the school organization concerning record keeping—can be overwhelming to the beginner.

How does one get help? There are two ways. It is either asked for or it is offered. Yet there is nothing accidental or obvious about either. The ways in which the teacher gets help are related to the formal and informal social organization of the school. Every school has its table of organization, and the members of that organization are arranged hierarchically. At the bottom are the teachers (although the children are below them), arranged according to length of experience, assignment to grade, and assignment to exponents along the grade, i.e., "better" through "poorer" classes. The beginner is very low in the scale and is closest in social relations to those with similar experience. Age, having been classmates, similar interests outside school, etc. may also influence this. The beginning teachers are often assigned to the middle or lower classes in the grade; substitutes with little experience or prestige get the bottom classes, while the top class on the grade goes to the more experienced, effective teacher and carries with it greater prestige. Recent pressure by teacher union groups have led to the adoption of rotation systems for the assignment to classes on the grade in some schools. However, prestige continues to be assigned to the "better" classes and teachers given the "poorer" classes expect to be rewarded with a more prestigious assignment the following year.

Above the teachers in the formal structure there is also professional staff, i.e., those assigned as co-ordinators and specialists. These positions carry greater prestige for the persons filling them, and these staff members are a little more distant from the teachers. Standing highest in the formal organization are the administrators, the assistant principal and the principal.

Every organization has its informal structure as well, and schools are no exception. Informal organization generally refers to the social relations that develop among the staff or workers above and beyond the formal relations set by the organization structure. Sometimes informal organization also refers to the actual relations between the formal structure and the pressures of the interpersonal relationships among the participants in the organization. Whereas formal organization refers usually to the pattern set by management, informal organization generally suggests peer groups and patterns of leadership within these groups.[1] In schools these informal

[1] Amitai Etzioni, *Modern Organizations,* Englewood Cliffs, N.J.: Prentice-Hall, 1964, p. 40.

Getting Help

social groupings develop among those with whom there is social contact or common interest, such as being alumni of the same college, joining the staff at the same time, working on the same grade level, sharing nearby rooms; even time of marriage and housefurnishing may form the basis of the association. Race, too, is an important factor in the establishment of informal social groups.

Help for the teacher comes through both the formal and the informal organization of the school. Let us examine the matter of pedagogical assistance. Almost all of the administrators met by the beginning teachers seem to be generous in their offers of help. However, their offers tend to be couched in general terms—"If there is anything you need or want to know, ask me." Unfortunately, new teachers are unlikely to define or know precisely what help they need. One of the earliest concerns they express is related to the matter of lesson planning. Where they are required to submit plans they do not seek the assistance of the administrators but turn instead to those in closer social relations to themselves, i.e., other beginning teachers. It appears that within the formal structure of the school the newcomer initiates interaction for assistance in pedagogical matters primarily with specialists and with those who are close to her in the social hierarchy of the school, other beginners. Help is also sought informally from other teachers with whom there is social contact or physical contact such as being close by in location in the building, sharing a lunch table, or participating in a motor pool for transportation together. The supervisors who stand in professional relationship to the teacher, i.e., consultants, co-ordinators, or master teachers, sometimes initiate the interaction with the beginners concerning professional assistance. This is appreciated by the teachers, and their help is accepted. Such persons are in the position of assisting the teacher without making judgments concerning her worthiness. Her relationship to them is based on professional colleague ties. However, despite her insecurity, the beginning teacher does come into the school with a generalized conception of what teaching should be like. Although these conceptions vary in detail, it is generally true that the beginner assumes that the specialist ought to be just that, a person expert in his area.

These norms concerning the specialist have been obviously flouted in the assignment of Mr. Lee as a reading specialist. As a consultant, the reading improvement teacher ought to be someone who commands professional authority in regard to reading. Although apparently assigned by the principal to this position as the lesser of two evils, it is necessary to understand that norms cannot be violated with impunity, despite the wide tolerance for actual behavior which does exist. The fundamental danger arising from flagrant violation of norms is that it breeds cynicism and can lead to deteriorating relations within the school organization, among both the teachers and the children.[2]

Administrators themselves are more distant from the beginning teacher than are either specialists or other teachers. When help is sought from the administration it is most likely to be in the case of supplies or in respect to discipline problems the teachers are having with children. Teachers in the early part of their careers seek the principal's or assistant principal's help in solving problems related to children the teacher views as causing difficulty and preventing her from teaching. She often wishes the problem child removed from the class, demoted to a lower class on the grade, helped by the guidance counselor or social agency, almost anything, but especially for the child to be removed, punished, prevented in one way or another from continuing to cause disturbance. An administrative solution is sought from the administration.

This tendency to seek the principal's assistance in matters of discipline rather than traditional pedagogy is sometimes misinterpreted by the administrators as indicating young teachers' lack of interest in improving their teaching. The latter is of prime concern to the teacher, but a professional discussion concerning a matter of pedagogy is usually not initiated by a beginning teacher with members of the administration. This may be the result of the beginner's fear of revealing herself as incompetent to the administration, which she assumes expects her to function without difficulty. On the other hand, she does not at first feel accountable for prob-

---

[2] George C. Homans, *The Human Group,* New York: Harcourt, Brace & Co., 1950, p. 123.

lem children in her classroom and feels free to seek help directly in this regard.

It does not take very long, however, for a teacher to learn that frequent requests for administrative assistance in dealing with children she finds disruptive mark her as one who is having difficulty in coping with her position and therefore displaying evidence of incompetence. In addition, it is not so simple a matter to have children removed from classes, especially for a beginner. Thus, teachers turn to the informal system for assistance. It is through the informal system, as well as through the formal system, that teachers learn the know-how of how to function on the job, how to deal with "difficult" children, skills of teaching, how to deal with the administration, parents, etc. In addition to actual instruction received through informal channels, the teacher receives support through the friendship and empathy of her colleagues. Thus, Mr. Julian, another teacher with no authority in the formal organization of the school, has provided a great deal of help concerning the planning of a lesson and also has provided moral support to a troubled beginner. Schools are filled with such unsung heroes who make it possible for young, inexperienced colleagues to learn their jobs and develop security within them, and who provide some of the most positive aspects of teacher education.

The importance of the informal channels of instruction for beginning teachers is extremely great, and its implications for the in-service education of teachers have been underemphasized. Certainly, if some of the finest teacher education can be given in this way, so can some of the worst. If the teachers in a school, for example, have been unsuccessful in providing positive educational experience for the children, it is through the informal as well as the formal organization of the school that the inadequate approaches are perpetuated. While formal structures may change, it is also necessary to pay attention to the norms passed on through the informal channels. This is not to imply that the informal structures ought to be destroyed. On the contrary, they are a normal part of group life. Their existence should be recognized and utilized constructively.

CHAPTER 16

The Saga of Class 1/5

Ideally, public schools exist to provide equal educational opportunity for all, and to provide opportunity for each to develop according to his capacity. The following excerpts, which follow the experience of a first-grade teacher and her class through the first semester, illustrate the way in which the bureaucratic structure of the school frustrates the attainment of ideal goals. This case indicates the way in which, through both informal and formal mechanisms, the teacher comes to accept the mores of the slum school, which tend to project the cause of school failure upon the children or their families and away from the school.

**Miss Seabold
Grade 1/5**

October 26. Mrs. Jones, the sixth-grade teacher, and I went on to discuss the problems of reading. I said, "I wonder about my children. They don't seem too slow; they seem average. Some of them even seem to be above average. I can't understand how they can grow up to be fifth- and sixth-grade children in school and still be reading on the second-grade level. It seems absolutely amazing."

Mrs. Jones explained about the environmental problems

The Saga of Class 1/5

that these children have. "Some of them never see a newspaper. Some of them have never been on the subway," she said. "The parents are so busy having parties and things that they have no time for their children. They can't even take them to a museum or anything. It's very important that the teacher stress books."

Mrs. Jones tells her class, "If anyone asks you what you want for Christmas, you can say you want a book." She told me that she had a 6/1 class last year and it was absolutely amazing how many children never even saw a newspaper. They can't read Spanish either. So she said that the educational problem lies with the parents. They are the ones that have to be educated.

It's just a shame that the children suffer. I guess this problem will take an awful lot to straighten it out. I guess it won't take one day or even a year; it will take time.

December 14. Here I am a first-grade teacher. I get a great thrill out of these children being able to read, but I often wonder, "Am I teaching them how to read or are they just stringing along sight words that they know?" I never had a course in college for teaching phonetics to children. In this school we have had conferences about it, but I really wish that one of the reading teachers would come in and specifically show me how to go about teaching phonics. I have never gotten a course like this and it is a difficult thing, especially when there is a language barrier and words are quite strange to these children who can't speak English. How can they read English? So we have a great responsibility on our shoulders, and teachers should take these things seriously.

January 4. Something very, very important and different has happened to me in my school. It all happened in the last week before the vacation, on Tuesday. Mr. Frost, our principal, came over to me and asked me if I would be willing to take over a second-grade class starting after the vacation. Well, I looked at him and I said, "Why?"

He told me briefly that the registers in the school have dropped and according to the Board of Education the school must lose a teacher. Well, apparently he was getting rid of a second-grade teacher and he wanted to combine two of the first-grade classes. The registers on the first grade were the lowest in the school, I believe. Anyway, he told me that he was going to all the afternoon first-grade teachers asking if any of them would be willing to change in the middle of the term. He said that he thought perhaps someone really would want it and, instead of his just delegating a person, it would be better if he asked each one individually.

I was torn between many factors. As you know, I enjoyed my class very, very much and I enjoy teaching the first grade. But because I was teaching afternoon session (our school runs on two different sessions) I was left out of many of the goings on within the school, as my hours were different, and it also sort of conflicted with my home responsibilities. Well, with these two points in mind, I really felt that I would rather stay with my class than to switch over in the middle of the term. But he explained further that some of the classes would not remain the same because there would be many changes made. So, being the type of person that I am, I felt that, even though I did want to stay with my class and the children and the first grade, if something had to be done in the school, there was no way of stopping it and I might as well do it. I explained to Mr. Frost that even though I wouldn't want to change in the middle—after all, it would be a whole new experience, two classes of children would be suffering by the change—but if it had to be done I would be willing to take on the new responsibility.

With that, Mr. Frost said, "Thank you," and said he would go around to the other teachers to see if anyone really wanted to change. Well, already I felt that it was going to be me, but I wasn't sure.

A little later on in the day I was taking my class to recess and we were lining up. We had just gotten into the hall. I had spoken to Miss Lane, another teacher, about what had happened. He had also spoken to her. She told me that she didn't quite understand what Mr. Frost was talking about, so I explained it to her in more detail. At that point Mr. Frost came over and spoke to me and told me that he was sorry but that I had been the one elected. Well, I said that I hoped that I would be able to do a good job, and that was that.

The Saga of Class 1/5

From that point on there was an awful lot of talk in the school. Everybody was talking about it, at least, everyone who knew something about the matter. So all the afternoon first-grade teachers and all the morning first-grade teachers knew and many of the new teachers (those that I came into the school with), and apparently there was a lot of business going on that I can't begin to describe because I don't know how the whole thing started in the first place. However, from the office I did find out that it wasn't Mr. Frost's fault or anything that the second-grade teacher was going to be dismissed. It was a directive from higher up that stated he would lose a teacher. How he chose this particular teacher to let go I really can't say. I understand that they really didn't get along too well and neither of them was too happy in the school working together.

Everything went so quickly and everybody was talking to me. Mrs. Parsons spoke to me. She is my assistant principal. She was supervisor of the first grade and she will be in charge of the second grade also. I was told that I would have to take over the new class on January 2, the first day that we return from the vacation. I really felt terrible about my children, but it was something that had to be done and I did it.

Thursday, Mr. Frost talked to the other afternoon teachers and myself. He referred to me as the hero and he said, "Now it is your turn to be heroes also." He asked the afternoon first-grade teachers if they would be willing to have their registers become higher by having my twenty-seven children split up among the four remaining afternoon classes, or did they think he should have them split up among all the first-grade classes, some of which met in the morning.

He was straightforward, saying that he didn't think it would be a good idea for the children to be split up among all the first-grade teachers. I agreed with him. He felt that it would be trying on the parents and on the children to have a whole new schedule worked out. After all, if you're used to going to school from twelve to four, coming to school from seven-thirty to twelve is quite a difference. It would be very, very hard on the parents. Especially in this neighborhood, where sometimes you have a few children in the same grade, a few in different grades. These parents do bring them to school and take them home. So I agreed with Mr. Frost. The other teachers didn't seem too happy about the idea, but they said they would go along with it.

Mr. Frost and Mrs. Parsons worked out a plan whereby the 1/1 class register would go up to thirty-five, which is generally what a 1/1 class has (thirty-four or thirty-five, I can't remember exactly), and the 1/3 class register would go up to thirty-two or thirty-three. And so forth down the line. Class 1/5 (my class) would be erased, and then came 1/7. Their register would go up to about thirty; and then came 1/9, which would go up to about twenty-six or so. The teachers didn't think it was so bad then, but we all did have added responsibilities.

Mr. Frost then added that if at this time we had any children in our classes that we felt did not belong, this was our chance to have them changed, since there would be many interclass transfers in order to make more homogeneous classes and he would be willing to grant these changes now. So we all had to sit down and think—"Who belongs? Who doesn't belong?"—and I, of course, had to decide where twenty-seven children would belong. I went through my class and divided them into groups to the best of my ability. I put them where I felt they would belong. In the 1/1 class, I put Joseph R., who scored the highest on the reading readiness test, and as a result of his score on the test and his work in class I felt Joseph did belong in the 1/1 class. Then again, I looked further and Lydia A., who I believe is a very smart girl and who wasn't really working as well as she could in my class, I felt she belonged in the 1/1 class. Lydia scored second highest on the reading readiness test. In the 1/1 class I also put Anita R. Anita is a bit older than the rest of the children, but she has caught on most beautifully to most phases of school work even though she just came to the United States last March. Also, she scored the same as Lydia on the reading readiness test.

Then I looked further and I decided that I would put Robert M. in the 1/1 class. I felt strongly that Robert was by far the best child in my class. Robert did every bit of the work ever assigned. He caught on very, very quickly to all phases of work besides doing his work well, quickly, efficiently, and neatly. Even though on the reading readiness he only scored in the fiftieth percentile, I felt he really stood out and *I also felt that once you're in a "1" class, unless you really don't belong, you have a better chance. For some reason the "1" class on the grade is really the only class that you would term a "good" class.* [Author's emphasis] So those four children I recommended for the 1/1 class.

Then I went down the line, and for the 1/3 class I picked nine children, really good children who on the whole listened and did their work. Most of them scored in the fiftieth and fortieth percentile on the reading readiness and they were coping with school problems very, very well. In the 1/7 class I put the slower children, and in the 1/9 class, of course, which is Mrs. Gould's, I put all the children that really weren't doing well in schoolwork at all. I think I should tell you some of the children that I placed in that class. First, of course, Alberto. Alberto is still not able to write his name, so he was in that class. Then I put Beatrice, Stella, Pedro, and several others who really were not working as well as the other children in the class.

I know that the other teachers do have a big job before them because whichever class these children are placed in will not have been doing exactly the same work. The children either have much to catch up on or they might review some of the work and the teachers will have to be patient either way. On the whole, I really don't think anyone will have serious discipline problems except perhaps in the 1/1 class where Lydia and Anita have been placed.

The time came when I had to tell the children that I would not be their teacher any more. Well, as young as they are I think that many of them caught on immediately and before I could say anything, faces were very, very long and the children were mumbling, "But I wanted you for a teacher."

That was all I needed! I felt even worse than I felt when I found out that I wouldn't be with them any more. So I continued talking and I told them that it's just something that happens and that I would still be in the school and maybe next year they would get me when they go to the second grade. I told them that I would miss them all, that they would have a lot of fun in their new classes and they would learn a lot. And, of course, I said, "You know all the other teachers. Some of you will get Mrs. Lewis. Some will get Miss Lane, some will get Miss Taylor, and some will get Mrs. Gould."

To my astonishment, Anita kept saying over and over, "But I want you for a teacher. But I want you for a teacher."

I looked around the room. Most of the children were sitting there with very, very long faces. Joseph C. was sitting there with the longest face you could imagine and Robert G. said he didn't want another teacher and all of a sudden Joseph started crying and just didn't stop. He cried all the way out into the hall when we got dressed to go home. I spoke to him softly and said, "Joseph, wouldn't you like Miss Lane for a teacher?" She was standing right near me and finally he stopped crying.

I said goodbye to them and that I would see them all. And that was the end of my class. . . .

. . . Good schools. Poor schools. What is a good school? Is a good school one that is in a good neighborhood, that has middle-class children? Is that a good school? Is a poor school one in a depressed area where you have Negro and Puerto Rican children? These are common terms that people refer to all the time. They hear your school is on Wolf Street—"Oh, you must be in a bad school."

I don't really think that that is what a good or a bad school is. I think a good school is a school that is well run, has a good administration, has people that work together well, has good discipline, and where the children are able to learn and also, of course, where there are numerous facilities for the children and the teachers. In my estimation a poor or a bad school would be one in which the administration and the teachers do not work together, are not working in the best interests of the children, and where learning is not going on. Also, a poor school is one where you don't have proper facilities. I am not acquainted with many of the public schools and I really can't say that the ones that I know are better or worse. I believe my school is a pretty good school. It isn't in the best neighborhood. There are many, many problems in my school, but on the whole I think that the teachers and the administration work together and I do believe that they are doing the best they can with the problems that are around.

You have to remember that in a school such as ours the children are not as ready and willing to learn as in schools in middle-class neighborhoods. [Author's emphasis]

DISCUSSION

Although the human being is born with the capacity to function within a social group, his position within it and the forms of behavior and beliefs appropriate to his particular culture have to be learned. Socialization is the name given to the process by means of which the individual is integrated into his society. It is through this process that the individual adapts to fellow members of his group and is assigned or achieves the various status positions he will assume during his lifetime. These can vary with sex, age, kinship, etc.[1]

Man must do an enormous amount of learning in order to achieve competency and acceptability in his culture. The process of learning the behavior and beliefs appropriate to the culture and to the position of the individual within it has been termed enculturation.[2] It is through this process that the individual's behavior falls well within the limits of tolerance established by the culture, for the individual internalizes the values and beliefs, becomes possessed of the necessary skills and techniques to function within the society, and becomes capable of adjusting and adapting to his physical and social environment.

Enculturation proceeds throughout one's lifetime, for although by adulthood one has usually learned the culture so well that he need give it little thought, an individual has continually to learn the behavior and attitudes appropriate to the new situations in which he finds himself. Thus, although already socialized and learned in the ways of the culture as a student in college, the potential teacher must learn principles, methods, and an ideal role in regard to teaching. As a teacher within a school, he or she must learn the appropriate behavior, attitudes, and skills required in the new situation.

---

[1] Melville J. Herskovitz, *Man and His Works*, New York: Alfred A. Knopf, 1949, p. 38.
[2] Ibid., pp. 39–40.

Much of this learning is conscious. Some of it is not. What is significant is that, while on the job, the teacher is also socialized, i.e., she is integrated into the ongoing society of the school, and, in addition, the teacher is learning the values, beliefs, and attitudes which in reality govern the functioning of the institution.

The saga of class 1/5 illustrates the manner in which one teacher internalized the cultural characteristics of the slum school in which she is working, coming to accept its organization and the prevailing rationale for pupil failure. There are many lessons here for administrators of inner-city schools. If they wish to change the pattern of failure in school in order to equip inner-city youngsters with the education to enable them to equitably participate in the opportunities provided by American society, they must become increasingly aware of the values and attitudes prevailing in the school milieu, as well as the educational implications of the organizational structure, for these conditions play a crucial role in the education of children.

The teacher of class 1/5 has warm, friendly relations with her youngsters. She respects and admires their abilities and is troubled by what she foresees in the future for them as she surveys the large amount of educational failure by the sixth grade evident in her school.

Very early in her teaching career, however, this new teacher is indoctrinated by a more experienced teacher in the belief, widely held, that the children come from inferior backgrounds and that it is the deficits in their homes—expressed here as being lack of newspapers and parental care—which prevent educational achievement. That the teachers and the school as an institution also operate as agents to ensure the failure of the children is never even implied or understood as a possible cause.

The beginning teacher, in her description of what happens to class 1/5, provides some insight into the genesis of failure that appears to be an almost inevitable consequence for most of the youngsters in the class.

First, their actual instruction should be examined. Early in her career, this new, very sincere teacher is painfully aware of her own deficits as a teacher. Unclear concerning her

The Saga of Class 1/5

teaching of so fundamental a subject as reading, she raises serious questions about how effectively she is providing instruction. As yet, she has not internalized the notion that the failure of children stems from gaps in their backgrounds. She is too sensitive concerning her own inadequacies and expresses a desire for professional growth in the teaching of reading. Although no consensus exists concerning reading methodology, the teacher is telling us that there are serious weaknesses in evaluation and feedback, so that she is unable to know what the children have really been taught and have learned.

By the end of the term, however, all this has changed. By that time, the prognosis for failure is positive. The school practically ensures the failure of the children, and the teacher has been socialized to rationalize this in terms of pupil inadequacy.

An examination of the case will give insight into how this takes place. First, as a result of the drop in school register, the principal loses a teacher, which means the loss of a class, leading to the distribution of one class of children among other classes. The principal and the teachers have little control over this phenomenon. They are themselves manipulated by forces outside their direct control. Education budgets, tables of organization, or directions from headquarters, create conditions without regard for the views and advice of those people in closest relation to the children themselves.

A drop in pupil registers would seem to imply the opportunity to provide for a higher adult-pupil ratio and, consequently, the opportunity for more individualized instruction and pedagogical supports for the youngsters and teachers in this school. Instead it led to the loss of a teacher, higher registers, and, perhaps most important, increased time spent by the administrator and his staff on the mechanics of administration rather than on educational supervision—less time spent on professional growth of teachers and on the education of the children. Why one teacher rather than another was released is unclear, though the substitute status and lower rank of the dismissed teacher was probably involved. As a result of this situation, many classes are disrupted, several first-grade class registers increase, time for instruction is lost, and concern is felt by teachers and pupils alike.

Another even more significant clue to possible eventual failure for the children is described in poignant detail by our teacher when she tells how the youngsters in her class will be distributed among the other first-grade classes. All educators have learned about different maturation rates for children, differential rates of learning readiness, and the developmental differences between boys and girls relevant to learning. To determine the educational outcome for youngsters at this early stage of their development, without due provision for understanding of these normal growth variations, would seem to be a travesty of the educational process. Yet here, in the first half of the first grade, a relatively inexperienced young teacher, herself keenly aware of her own deficiencies as an educator, is placed in the position of literally deciding the educational future of her charges. A few are selected for success—"I felt that once you're in a '1' class, unless you really don't belong, you have a better chance. For some reason the '1' class on the grade is really the only class that you would term a 'good' class." Several children are placed in a class labeled "slow." The other youngsters are relegated to a state of limbo, and the middle range does not carry with it the hope of providing a "better chance."

Thus, before these youngsters have completed four months of schooling, their educational futures have been "tracked," for all through the grades the labels of their class placement will follow them, accompanied by teacher attitudes concerning their abilities. Some youngsters are selected very early for success, others written off as slow. The opportunity to move across is limited, for differential teaching occurs and helps to widen the gap between children. In addition, the children too become aware of the labels placed upon them. Their pattern for achievement in later years is influenced by the feelings of success or failure in these early school experiences.

As she reflects upon what a "good" school or a "bad" school is, our teacher continues to include the learning by children as a significant criteria, together with good relations between staff and administration. The children in the school in which she works do not achieve academically. When de-

The Saga of Class 1/5

scribing whether or not her own school is "good" or "bad" she stresses the good relations between the administration and the teachers. That the children do not learn does not now seem so important, for ". . . the children are not as ready and willing to learn as in schools in middle-class neighborhoods."

How well the teacher has internalized the attitude that child deficits explain the failure of children to succeed in school. How normal she now considers the administrative upheavals and their effects upon teachers and children. How perfectly ordinary she considers the tracking of youngsters so early in their school years. The teacher of class 1/5 has been socialized by the school to accept its structure and values. She is not likely to effect much change in the prognosis of failure for most of the children in this school, because she has come to accept the very structural and attitudinal factors which make failure nearly certain. In addition, with all the good intentions in the world, she has come to operate as an agent in the process of determining the life chances of the children in her class by distributing them as she does among the ranked classes on the grade.

This teacher came to her position with very positive impulses. She thought highly of her youngsters and was disturbed that, with what appeared to be good potential, there was so much failure in the school in the upper grades. She looked inward for ways in which she might improve her professional effectiveness in order to forestall retardation, and was not repelled by the neighborhood in which she worked. There is every indication that she had the potential of becoming a very desirable teacher of disadvantaged youngsters. However, her impulses were not enough. Unarmed with the strength that understanding the social processes involved might have given her, as well as having little power within the school hierarchy, this young teacher was socialized by the attitudes of those around her, by the administration and by the availability of a suitable rationale to explain her and the school's failure to fulfill ideal roles. As a result she came to accept traditional slum school attitudes toward the children, and traditional attitudes toward school organization as the way things have to be. She gives every indication of being a pleasant, flexible, co-operative young woman to have on one's staff. But at the same time, she has learned to behave and think in a way that perpetuates a process by which disadvantaged children continue to be disadvantaged.

CHAPTER 17

The Christmas Party: A Rite of Intensification

For young children there are evident disturbances in the classroom group during periods of impending interruption of the interaction between pupils and pupils and their teacher which come with vacation time. A ceremony, or rite of intensification, helps to renew or intensify the interaction among the members of the class to help restore equilibrium and improved group functioning.

Miss Bower
Grade 3/5

January 4. We had a rather nice Christmas party on Friday afternoon before vacation with candy and ice cream. Two of the mothers were very nice. They brought in cakes they had baked for the class, and some of the mothers had made Kool-Aid, etc., so we all pooled our resources and we had a party. We had a grab bag and I had gotten little gifts for each of the children, more or less little readers with stories. Most of them were Christmas stories: *The Little Snowman, Baby's First Christmas,* etc. The children had been going to the library, but I feel it's just as important that they read at home. I felt that something like this was on an easy enough level for them to read at home. There were cute stories, stories that they would enjoy, and I think that they were quite pleased by the whole thing and they really seemed to enjoy themselves.

We had music and we sang some Christmas songs and, of course, the grab bag was very exciting. I blindfolded them and every time someone pulled something out of the grab bag, there were "oohs" and "ahs."

Then came the big choice. I had lined up all the books on the window. They were all wrapped and the children went up and picked them out. They all looked identical, but the big decision was which one they should pick for themselves, and it was cute and they enjoyed themselves.

We also had art decorations, pictures, a Christmas poem, and I had them read Christmas stories. We sang Christmas songs and we wrote our Christmas experience charts story. The room was decorated with Santa Clauses and Christmas cards and we had made the grab bag look like a chimney. We used the brick-type crepe paper so that the room was really bedecked and looked very Christmasy. We all really enjoyed ourselves, including myself.

I really got a kick out of the children, the way they were dancing, etc. To me, I think they are wonderful because children have more rhythm, and they were really great. We all had a good time.

Miss Kooper
Grade 6/3

January 4. I guess the most important sequence of events is that my class was getting terrible, and I just couldn't wait for the vacation to come, because I figured that if I didn't get out of that room soon, that was going to be the end of me. All the teachers were having Christmas parties before the holiday, and I didn't think that I wanted to have my Christmas party because I just didn't think that the kids deserved it, and I didn't want them to think that they could behave any way they wanted and still have me turn around and say, "Okay, kiddies, I don't mind. I'll make your Christmas party anyway."

So I told them, "If your behavior doesn't improve, you are not getting any Christmas party." Their behavior didn't improve, so I said, "I am sorry, we are not going to have anything." They said they didn't care, they would have a party when they got home. But they could see that they were the only class that was not having a party so they were sort of upset.

The Friday before the end of school I saw all the kids walking in with little presents and I just wanted to die. I felt so bad. I was glad that the night before I had bought some little candies and some candy canes, and little dolls for Christmas presents; I had made a little package for each one of them. I figured that at three o'clock I would walk around and put one at each desk to show that I still thought enough about them to get them something for Christmas. When I saw them walking in with all their little presents I was glad that I had done this.

I received about seven or eight presents. I was very surprised and I felt bad that they had brought them, because I didn't appreciate the things that they gave me and took their money to buy.

Of course, they were very wild in the afternoon because they were the only class that was doing any work. Every other class was having Christmas parties and we could hear the music and dancing and here I am trying to teach a reading lesson. It didn't go too well.

At about a quarter to three I walked around and I put the little packages on each child's desk and when I came to Jose's desk he said, "I don't want it!" So I left it there anyway and he said, "I don't want it!" And then I went around and I came to Thomas and he said, "I don't want it!" And I walked away and he said, "No, I don't want it." So I took it away from him. So that was that—we are sort of mutual enemies.

And the presents that they gave me—I got two half-slips that were really nice and bath soap. One girl gave me perfume, forty-nine cents, Woolworth's original. It was so terrible, but I guess I will have to wear it just one time.

Rita Norris—I don't think I mentioned her too much in the course of the year—she's not any special problem. She's not a bad girl and she's not an exceptionally good girl. She's not very smart but she tries hard and she studies. She had said that she was getting me a present, and she came in in the morning but she didn't have anything. Most of the other girls put their presents on the desk and obviously she felt bad or she felt funny that she didn't bring a present. Of course, I didn't want anybody to feel bad and I didn't open the presents while the kids were there or anything. But that afternoon Rita came walking in and put a paper bag tied with a ribbon on my desk. I put it away and when I was going home I opened it up. It was one of her blouses. A blouse that she had worn. I could tell. It was dirty and creased. I looked at it and almost cried. I felt very terrible. She had felt bad that she didn't have a present and she had given me one of her own blouses. It just so happens that I have the same exact blouse. It's my own, so I brought the blouse back and I will give it back to her. I have it in the closet and I keep forgetting to give it to her. Besides the blouse, she gave me about two yards of material neatly folded up, a sort of green and blue printed material with a rough edge. And then she had a card. I could tell that it was a part of a large card or a game or something. She had cut out a picture of a reindeer. It's Christmasy and she gave it to me.

I really felt terrible.

Miss Peters
Grade 4/3

January 4. On Wednesday afternoon before Christmas vacation I had a party with my class. I told them that they could bring in any candy if they wished. They didn't have to but if they wanted to they could bring in candy for the party. And I told them that we were going to have a grab bag and I explained this to them. I told them that they weren't allowed to spend more than ten cents on a gift. And I said if they wanted to, the best gift would be to make something themselves, but I told them that every gift must be wrapped and we will place it in a big bag and then each person will come up—one at a time—and pick a surprise present. We did this and it was very successful.

At about two o'clock on Wednesday afternoon I gave out colored napkins with paper plates with Christmas designs on them and I had borrowed some decorations from the library to hang up on the walls. And I had bought several decorations myself. I bought a big Christmas sign which I hung on the

The Christmas Party: A Rite of Intensification

blackboard and then I bought a tree which we had decorated that week. Some of the children had brought in their own little Christmas cards which we put around it and tinsel which we put on it. This was a paper tree which opens up in three dimensions, and also we had a little snowman which is also a three-dimensional paper model.

I had my guitar in school that afternoon and we sang songs—songs that I had taught them before. The children enjoyed the guitar very much. Candy was given out and we sang Christmas songs and we had the grab bag and we played a few other games. We had arranged the room in a horseshoe setting. The regular arrangement of the classroom is in a semi-horseshoe, but now we arranged it to go all around the room and I think that the children reacted very nicely. They were very excited and they enjoyed it very much.

Also before the party, we had spoken about the week before—I spoke to them about the importance of giving anything—the joy of giving gifts—how that joy can be greater than receiving gifts—and then I said to them . . . I said, for example, "What do you think that the best gift that you could give me would be?" And one little boy said, "A pair of stockings." Which was very funny because I told him that that's really not what I wanted. I said what I wanted from them was to show me that they were grown up and they wanted to work and they did their homework every day and that they paid attention in class.

Mrs. Bender
Grade 5/2

January 4. As far as Christmas was concerned, I was out on Friday, I was ill, and I had planned to give them a Christmas party and I bought candy and prepared songs for them. But that morning I felt ill and I just could not gather myself to leave the house, so I called in and told the superintendent that I would be absent and please to see if she could get a substitute, which is what she did.

I went back to sleep. At eleven o'clock I got up and I thought I was feeling much better, so I called the school and told them I would be in to give the children their Christmas party. Would it be all right if I were to go to the classroom or should I leave the candy in the office? The clerk wanted to know if I wanted to speak to the principal, and he said it would be all right if I went up to the classroom, which is what I did.

I got to the school at a quarter to twelve and lo and behold, Philip Jones, the worst behavior problem in my class, had seen me walking out of a cab and had taken a pass and had waited for me downstairs. So he was my greeting committee. Just what I needed! I had a big box of candies individually wrapped for the children—each child in the class. He wanted to know if I had cake and I said, "No, Philip, it's not cake." He said, "May I tell everybody you're here?" And I said to him, "Please don't." I said, "Don't tell anyone until I come up after lunch. I don't want anyone to know I'm here and it's your secret and mine." He said, "All right." I asked the substitute teacher later, but he had not told any of the children in the class that he had seen me, which surprised me no end.

Well, anyway, I had had lunch in school and I was feeling ill again, so I brought the candy up to the class and I told them I wished them a Merry Christmas and a Happy New Year and I told them to be careful. They should be careful crossing streets and not to play with things that might hurt them. That was the extent of the Christmas party, except that it was very nice.

DISCUSSION

Just as individuals in the course of their lifetimes must readjust to changed relationships with others, so groups of people do not maintain an even pace of interaction with one another, but experience periods of disturbance. Frequently these changes have been associated with the variations in season, climate, day and night. Thus, among agricultural people the harvest and the planting seasons mark periods of change in human activity, and the consequent change in interaction among the people performing certain functions, and these have usually been marked by ceremonial observance.

The Christmas Party: A Rite of Intensification

The ceremonies which accompany the life crises of individuals were termed *rites of passage* by van Gennep.[1] Further refining the concept of rites of passage, Eliot D. Chapple and Carleton S. Coon termed the ceremonies associated with groups *rites of intensification*.[2]

Changes in activity or interaction rates among members of a group represent crises which threaten group stability, and rites of intensification serve to reinforce or to intensify the relations among members, helping to preserve the group and enabling it to retain continuity.[3] The ceremonies accompanying these periods of change can take place at various times. Some rites of intensification mark the end of a period of activity, some mark the beginning. The ceremonies themselves have been described as providing a dramatic representation of the habitual relationships of the individuals in the sets of which the system is composed:

> *This acting out of the ordered interaction of the members has the effect of reinforcing or intensifying their habitual relations, and thus serves to maintain their conditioned responses. That is why we have called them Rites of Intensification.*[4]

Also accompanying rites of intensification there is generally a wealth of symbolism, helping to reinforce the ordered relationships among the members of the group to one another.

In general, then, these rites, coming periodically, help to reinforce the habitual relations within the group or society, and their relative elaboration is a function of the gravity of the disturbance which it is their purpose to allay.

All of us are familiar with rites of intensification. Some of these are imbedded in religious context, others are quite secular in nature. The annual family gathering for Thanksgiving dinner, for example, serves to bring together in ordered

---

[1] Arnold van Gennep, *The Rites of Passage,* Chicago: The University of Chicago Press, 1960.
[2] Eliot D. Chapple and Carleton S. Coon, *Principles of Anthropology,* New York: Henry Holt & Company, 1942, p. 398.
[3] Ibid.
[4] Ibid., pp. 507–8.

relationship people who might otherwise so decrease their interaction with one another as to leave the group and lose identity with the extended family. This ceremony also reinforces a feeling of common heritage and nationhood to all Americans. The annual banquet, the convention, and the office Christmas party[5] all serve as rites of intensification.

Within the school, there are also periods of fluctuation in regard to the interaction of the people within it. Awareness of these fluctuations, sensitivity to their significance, and provision for the re-establishment of equilibrium are highly significant things. Most school people are generally aware that there are periods during which it seems to be more difficult to work with children than others. Teachers speak of the children being "jumpy," "nervous," "difficult to handle." These symptoms seem to be greatest before holidays, on Friday afternoons, during periods of marked climatic change or weather change—rain, snow, spring—and particularly during teacher absence. Sometimes these changes come so often that children are difficult all the time and stability becomes almost impossible to obtain. Ordinarily, however, there are periods of fluctuation, and these have to do with changes in interaction. For example, Fridays precede the weekend, during which time there is ended interaction with the teacher and classmates in the classroom setting, and increased interaction with others—family, peers, etc.—outside of school. The restiveness of children is in part a response to the termination of the classroom relations and the preparation for the taking up of new ones.

The disbanding of the group for the weekend, however, is not very serious, and Monday morning arrives quickly enough, with the re-establishment of group relations accompanying it. Longer holidays, however, and a high incidence of teacher absence are more serious in the threat that they pose to the group. For young children especially, these disruptions take on even greater significance, for the disbanding of the group and the loss of the teacher can appear to be so final.

---

[5] Recent decline in the importance attached to office Christmas parties may be related to increasing concern with individual careers as opposed to company loyalty.

The Christmas Party: A Rite of Intensification

The Christmas vacation is the first really long holiday of the school year. Thanksgiving, important as it is, is much more brief, and generally easy to celebrate, for its secular nature is clear and it is practiced fairly uniformly in the nation. Christmas, however, is a more difficult holiday to celebrate within schools, for the history of Christmas is involved with both religious and secular traditions, and Christmas serves as a rite of intensification for the family and for the religious community as well, causing many sources of stimulation and many accompanying reordering of relationships for the children and the teacher. The children are undergoing a particularly disturbing period at this time. Their school routine with its ordered relations between pupils and teachers is coming to a halt, various degrees of heightened activity with others is coming into being, i.e., with church, family, friends outside of school. All kinds of stimulations in regard to change of activity affect the children: shopping, advertising, family preparations for celebrations, etc.

It is, of course, true that whether or not to celebrate Christmas in school is a highly controversial matter. The problem is enormously complicated by its involvement with relations of church and state in regard to public education, the handling of a religious theme in a secular manner, the existence of many non-Christian teachers, and the presence of non-Christian children. It is not the purpose of this discussion to explore these very important considerations. The emphasis here is rather on the significance of behavioral difficulties before a holiday, whether the holiday is termed Christmas, or winter recess, or anything else, as well as on the significance of an activity to renew group equilibrium.

Most important for the teacher is the fact that the classroom situation and her relations with the children are coming to an end for a period of time. This represents potential danger to the group, and the children as well as the teacher are aware of the impending holiday and cognizant of the tensions and excitement associated with it. The children and the teacher, preparing for their holiday from school, also exhibit the slackening of relations and involvement with each other which makes discipline and order so difficult to maintain at this time. These symptoms of disorder and jumpiness are to be anticipated. They are responses to the impending breakdown in the relations among the members of the group.

The rite of intensification serves the highly significant and useful purpose of reinforcing the ordered interaction between pupils and teacher, providing them with reinforcement of their habitual relations with one another in the classroom, despite the absence from one another they will experience. The opportunity to intensify their habitual relations serves to reinforce the pupil-teacher relationship, providing the opportunity to intensify the relations between pupil and teacher, bringing them into more active relationship with one another, after they have maintained very distant relationship.

The incidents described by these teachers illustrate these points. Of course, the specific content of the Christmas party varies from class to class, although certain things appear in common. On the whole, traditional decorations, secular in nature, dominate the scene. Red, green, tinsel, evergreens, Santa Claus and reindeer, candy, and gift-giving are typical. Singing and dancing, jokes, and grab bags; a spirit of gaiety prevails. Successfully carried out, the Christmas party serves to give the teacher a warm, happy feeling in regard to her class, helping to ensure her readiness to return at the end of vacation, and the children too are left with a happy, warm feeling for their teacher, who has indicated to them her regard for them. Symbolic of the relationship between pupil and teacher is the gift-giving which takes place. The giving of gifts at Christmas stems from the Christmas tradition as well, but it takes on a special meaning for the teacher and pupil in the class.

Some teachers are more talented in relation to party-giving than others. But one does not have to be a skilled entertainer or hostess to ensure a successful rite of intensification. The most essential ingredients are a recognition of the seriousness of the matter and its implication for renewing or reviving group interaction and harmony, and preparation for the event which takes into account the nervousness and excitement of the children and their need to be helped through this period without recrimination and denigration. Thus, the teacher who provides opportunity for the children to make gifts, prepare a grab bag for classmates, participate in entertainment, dec-

The Christmas Party: A Rite of Intensification

orating the room, etc. helps to channel the energies of the youngsters and direct them to increased interaction with herself and with one another. In deprived areas, expense in relation to Christmas looms as a problem. For this reason many school systems forbid gift-giving to the teacher. However, for many children the giving of a gift to the teacher symbolizes their willingness to interact with her. For some children the giving of a gift represents presentation of themselves as significant persons. For these reasons provision might be made for children to make their own gifts, or some substitute in the form of service for the class party or behavior in regard to the teacher should be encouraged.

Just as a successful Christmas party can serve a valuable function as a rite of intensification, so an unsuccessful one or the absence of one can create serious problems for the group. It is interesting to note the case of the teacher who felt too ill to come to school the day of the Christmas party. Despite her illness she felt impelled to come to school to demonstrate her attachment to her class. It is interesting too that her most difficult behavior problem took this opportunity to greet her and to demonstrate his willingness to follow her request that he keep her presence a secret. Here is illustrated the opportunity provided by rites of intensification for the establishment of relationships on a more intense level than before. This child was demonstrating to the teacher his acceptance of her authority and his desire to belong.

The second anecdote demonstrates nearly complete breakdown of interaction between teacher and pupils, with serious danger to the continuity of the group evident. This teacher admits to being ready to resign. The excitement and disorder in her class before Christmas is interpreted by her as misbehavior challenging to her authority, and, unable to understand its relationship to the closing of school, she takes the position of punishing or denying to the children the ceremonial celebration that every other class in the school is performing. Obviously, this has disastrous results. Her attempts to carry on a reading lesson when the class has already psychologically disbanded meet with complete failure.

Having given the children rather obvious evidence that she too has psychologically left the class, the teacher cannot recoup by the perfunctory gift-giving at the close of the day. This has come too late for some children, and they do not recognize the gift as truly representing their teacher's involvement and concern for them. Thus, it is not surprising that some children refuse to accept her presents. Some children need more genuine evidence of the teacher's willingness to establish teacher-pupil relations with them. Other children, for a variety of reasons, require less. How embarrassed this teacher feels when she realizes that some of the children are concerned enough and interested enough to present her with gifts as symbols of their acceptance of the relationship. Yet the teacher's lack of respect for the youngsters and her inability to relate to them with warmth and dignity is indicated by her derogatory comments concerning their gifts. This teacher has almost literally walked out on her class—many children feel that she has done this even though physically present—and several children seek to act out a rite of intensification to bind their teacher to them via the traditional and symbolic giving of gifts.

Unless the significance of the Christmas party is seen in terms of the renewal and intensification of interaction relationships in a period of group crisis, and as a technique for re-establishing equilibrium, opportunity for the incorporation of members and the ordered structuring of the classroom can be lost. To treat the Christmas party in terms of reward and punishment, to punish children for responding to changes in interaction patterns, rather than understanding and channeling the nervousness and disorder which may accompany this, is to run the risk of abetting the destruction of the group. This can lead to the loss of children to learning, and the loss of teachers to teaching.

The Christmas vacation is clearly preceded by a period of excitement which accompanies the anticipated closing of school and subsequent halting of interaction between the members of the class and the school community. Nonetheless, it is but one period during the school year in which the interaction of the pupils and teachers is so threatened that a rite of intensification is needed to renew equilibrium. Fluctuations occur throughout the year, and may vary from school to school, area to area. On the whole, however, holidays, the end of examination periods, approaching graduations are among those times that present crises to the group and lend themselves to a breakdown of order.

Schools frequently provide rites to restore equilibrium. The Monday morning or Friday afternoon assembly program, for example, is one such device. Unfortunately, there is sometimes little cognizance taken of these inevitable increases and decreases in group interaction rates leading to problems of order and discipline in school. Also, the ceremonies have come to be perfunctory and are often held with little awareness of the significance their timing has on group behavior. Thus, in large crowded urban school systems, operating on several sessions, it becomes difficult to plan activities especially suited for time of day and place during the week or term. It also becomes easy to blame disorder upon individuals or sources outside the school's control. Sensitivity to changes in group behavior related to the problem of social interaction may prove to be of value to administrators. Their leadership can help to provide the necessary restoration of equilibrium, for they are in a position to plan school activities which can act to intensify or renew group functioning.

Ceremonies, ritual behavior—the party, assembly, Monday morning opening exercise, Friday afternoon reading and discussing time, etc.—if not treated in a perfunctory manner, and if timed with sensitivity to threats to group interaction, are not frills that are unimportant. All schools have their rhythm of activity which is highly significant and ought therefore to be studied and understood.

Living in a heterogeneous, changing, and secular society as we do, the rhythm of school activities sometimes conflicts with demands for increased interaction made upon children and teachers by forces outside the school. Ordinarily, in the past a school vacation was just that, an absence of school relations and attachments (a scheduled period during which activity is suspended). Just as school activity has ended, so does the opportunity for increased activity in relation to friends and family present itself. However, in recent years, the school has demanded more and more of the child's time and energies, and regards familial demands on children as competitive, where these do not coincide with the school's goals. For example, in some situations homework over weekends and over holidays commands continuous attachment to school on the part of the child, and prevents fully relaxed participation in family reunions, trips, parties, etc. Sometimes there is conflict over whether a child ought to devote his time to school, family, or the interaction with peers. These conflicting demands for the child's attention may have significant effects upon his relations with one or another group.

It may not be possible in the future for schools to decrease to any extent their demands on children; on the contrary, the likelihood is that demands will increase. Certainly major holidays, such as Christmas, when filled with term papers, book reports, etc., serve to bind the student to school and help decrease the attachments to family and peers. The implications of this for family life in general and social development of the child in particular remain to be examined. For older children and young people, there has come to be a blurring of those periods when school ends and school begins.

For young children in particular, there are evident disturbances in the group during periods of impending interruption of the interaction among pupils and between pupils and their teacher which comes with vacation time. A ceremony to renew or intensify the interaction of the members of the class or school helps to restore equilibrium and provides for improved group functioning. For this reason the Christmas party as here described is such an important event.

CHAPTER 18

School Boycott

Teachers and their supervisors working in situations affected by major social and political issues, such as school integration or community control, are increasingly troubled by the conflict they see between professional concerns and political decisions over which they have no control. Prior to the growth of militant pressures upon schools, many found it difficult to believe that the parents of their pupils cared enough to demand changes in school organization.

Miss Cedar
Grade 4/2

January 11. I really haven't given that much thought to my personal reactions to the threatened boycott because I just don't feel that it is going to come off. And if there is a boycott, it will affect my school, but I don't know how many parents would keep their children out, and as far as it goes for myself, I would go into school and I would continue teaching whoever is in my room. I think that most of the children would be there. Perhaps one or two, maybe a few more, would not, but I think the majority of them would be there.

There is one Puerto Rican teacher in the school who is the Spanish auxiliary teacher, and there are about six Negro teachers in the school. I have not discussed the boycott with them, nor with any of the other teachers in the school, so I can't tell you how they feel about it.

**Miss Seabold
Grade 1/5**

January 11. How do I feel about the threatened boycott? Well, I really don't know. Sometimes I'm for it and sometimes I'm against it, and I don't really think it will affect my school, but it might. I know the majority of them are Puerto Rican, but there might be some people outside since we do have about 20 per cent Negro pupils, and many of the Negroes in this school, you know, are strong members of the various organizations. Even in my new class on the guidance data, their former teacher left a little note about James B. and she said, "Do not hit under any circumstances. NAACP." So it might affect the school. As for my class, I guess it won't affect it too much. I have not discussed this with any of the other teachers and I don't know how they feel about it either.

**Mrs. Bender
Grade 5/2**

January 11. As far as the boycott is concerned, I don't think that this boycott will affect my school. They might have one or two pickets but I doubt very much if first of all if it will come off, or if it will go further. But as far as the boycott itself, our school is pretty well integrated, Negro and Puerto Rican, and I think actually what the NAACP and CORE are looking for is to integrate the all-Negro school, and since my class is mainly Puerto Rican and the school is mainly Puerto Rican, 55 per cent Puerto Rican and let's say 44 per cent Negro, and the remaining percentage white or other, that there will not be too much of an effect on the school.

There is one Puerto Rican teacher in the school. She is a Spanish auxiliary teacher. She hasn't been in school since Christmas. She's in the hospital now with an appendicitis attack. There are two Negro teachers in the school. We have not touched on this with the two Negro teachers, for the simple reason that one teacher is in the higher echelons of the

School Boycott

NAACP and takes everything personally, and everyone is afraid to approach her and discuss things with her, and the other teacher is a very emotional woman, and rather than upset her, we just avoid any talk about it at all.

And as far as I am concerned, I haven't heard anything discussed with the other teachers as far as this boycott is concerned. I don't know how they feel or I haven't heard the word boycott used in the school yet, and I personally feel that it won't be carried through.

Miss Kooper
Grade 6/3

January 11. As far as the boycott of the school is concerned, it really doesn't affect me one way or another. Even if it does take effect in the rest of the schools I don't think my school will be affected at all because the parents of the kids in my school don't want their kids home. They wouldn't keep them home on a matter of principle, I don't think. I really don't think they would do it. They would send them to school. Something as abstract as integration and as abstract as some of the ideals of the NAACP just don't—I don't think these people understand or are willing to even be bothered with anything like this. I really don't think that even if it does come through that it will have any effect on my school and my class.

If it does, how will I feel? I don't know. It's very non-educational to say it, but if many of them are out, it's just that much less that I have problems with. Very unethical, but . . . as far as I'm concerned, if they want to stay home and they believe in this, let them stay home. They'll lose a lot of work and it's ridiculous for them. They're so far behind anyway that they are going to stay out and miss more days of school! They're not going to benefit by it. If they want to stay home, let them stay home.

No, I haven't discussed the boycott at all. The only time I even heard it mentioned was when we had a grade conference and the assistant principal was talking about having clubs on Friday afternoons. He said we are going to start this program in the beginning of February if nothing happens with the boycott, and this is the only statement that I have heard.

There are five Negro teachers in this school. But I haven't talked with any of them or any of the teachers about the boycott. I don't know how they feel. Let the children stay home. If they want to stay home, let them stay home.

**Miss Harris
Grade 2/6**

January 11. I don't think if there is a boycott, it will affect my class or myself any more than any other class or any other teacher in the school, since the classes are pretty much evenly broken up into ethnic groups. The school is predominantly Puerto Rican with a Negro population of—I might say of about one quarter. There hasn't been any discussion at all about the boycott, except in a joking manner of the fact that the only holidays we have during this coming term are Easter and Lincoln's birthday, so that if it happens, it happens, and it's a nice day off. However, I think that this is in a half-joking tone, and if anything actually comes of it, this won't be the true feeling of the teachers. I don't know about this, but you know, when we get tired we say that will be a nice day to have off, but if we really got into a serious discussion, I think this wouldn't be the motive behind it and the thinking of the teachers.

**Miss Winters
Grade 2/4**

January 11. Are there any Negro or Puerto Rican teachers in my school? Quite a bit. Have I discussed it with them? No. How do they feel? I don't know. How do other teachers feel? I don't know. I'm sorry, I don't have this information. I feel that's just something that I don't talk about. Now, Miss Thomas is a Negro. I may not have mentioned that before, but she is and I would not bring that up with her. If she brought it up with me I would, but I would never say, "Well, how do you feel about the boycott?" because I feel that if she wanted to talk about it she would mention it to me, because that is the type of person Miss Thomas is. I feel about

School Boycott

the whole problem of segregation and integration in this school . . . it's such a terrible thing that the children who go to school and have so many other problems and who have to learn and everything—that they should be subjected to this. I don't know. I don't know the answers to the question. I guess if I did I'd probably go to Washington and solve the whole problem, but I do think that we live in a time where problems are pressing and hard and on top of all this it's terrible. Now, my school is not an integrated school. It's segregated. It's Negro 85 per cent, Puerto Rican 15 per cent. Now where is integration there? But is it fair to bring children on a bus ride for an hour, to bus them into that school to make it integrated? Is it fair to do that? Is it fair to make my children lose an hour of instruction to take them up to a school where they would be integrated? Is it fair to either side? Will this time come out of the learning time or will they have to be up so early in the morning that by two o'clock they are so tired—little ones? These are the questions I ask myself, and I say, "Oh, what is going to happen?"

I'm so deeply concerned about it and yet there is nothing I can do. I'll just sit back and wait and see what they are going to decide. Naturally, whatever they decide I probably will have to go along with. But I do hope that something happens that will solve it and make it all nice and all right.

Miss Bower
Grade 3/5

January 11. As far as the threatened boycott of the school in February, I am really afraid that this will certainly affect my school and the schools within the area I am teaching. I myself do not feel that I would stay out. I am sure I would go in. I don't think that the boycott is right. I don't think that it should be done. I don't think the basis for which they are going out is a valid one, etc. I feel that the teachers are doing as good a job as they can. I know that I myself am trying, and I am sure that all the other teachers in the area are trying to give these children as good an education as it is within their means to give them.

First of all, I don't think integration will ever really occur.

It just seems to me like an impossibility. I don't even hold for this bussing in of children in the open enrollment program myself. I feel that if you can get good teachers, the supplies that you need, etc., these children are going to learn, and they will learn just as well in, shall we say, a school that is made up of one racial group, etc.

The only thing that concerns me is the feelings of the other teachers in this school, what their reactions are to it, etc. Quite a few of the teachers in this school are Negro, and I might say perhaps one third. And as yet we really have not discussed this to any great extent. But we'll see. I really don't think I will stay out. But I mean, this is something that we're going to eventually have to discuss amongst ourselves and see what everyone's reactions are and really look at all sides of the picture, but I myself really do not hold it as something constructive. I really feel it is a very unnecessary thing.

Miss Devan
Grade 3/2

January 11. Boycott in February? I am still sort of in the middle. I believe in education and I know one of the leaders in the civil rights movement came out with the point that it's better for the children to get an education and to stay in school than to boycott the schools, that they shouldn't become involved in this. I think he has a point. But I also can see the other side of the coin where the minority groups want their rights, and they want their voice to be heard, and that one way that they could do this is by boycotting the schools, so I haven't reached any decision about which is better, boycott or come in to school. I guess boycott has more weight in one side of my mind because it is a definite action, a definite move toward expressing yourself. I don't know how effective it would be though, I really don't.

There are two Negro teachers in my school, Louise and Ada, but I haven't talked to them. I don't think we have any other Negro teachers. Puerto Rican teachers, I don't think so. No, there's none. But I haven't talked about this, and as a matter of fact, I think I will mention this to Ada when I talk to her.

Miss Hanes
Grade 3/4

January 11. About the boycott in February, I have a feeling that the boycott will not go through just as the proposed boycott in September did not go through—and I have the feeling, and of course it's only a feeling, that there will be another postponement, that some type of promise will be made, perhaps by the Board of Education to set up some type of integration timetable. I don't know that this will be the case, but I just have a feeling that it's going to happen.

DISCUSSION

On February 4, 1964, scarcely three weeks after these teachers commented on an impending school boycott called to demand the implementation of programs to achieve school integration, 464,361 pupils, or 44.8 per cent of the total enrollment of over one million pupils in the New York City public schools, stayed out of school. The absence rate in the districts in which the schools where these teachers taught were located ranged from 46.9 per cent to 92 per cent. The problem had not disappeared, the wished-for resolution had not arrived, and the schools were affected.

Nor was this the only boycott to confront the city school system. One year later, another was held, although participated in by fewer persons.[1] In addition, a counterboycott led by whites opposed to the bussing of children and the redistricting of schools to achieve integration was called. Throughout the nation's largest Northern urban centers, school boycotts to protest Northern *de facto* segregation, i.e., segregation due to the requirement that children attend their neighborhood schools, leading to segregated schools within the ghetto areas of the cities, took place. Massive educational failure within the *de facto* segregated schools had become evident, and increasingly the people of the inner city were viewing the schools

[1] See Estelle Fuchs, *Pickets at the Gates*, New York: The Free Press—The Macmillan Co., 1966, for a description of these boycotts.

as providing inferior educational opportunities for their children.

In the face of widespread unrest and obvious dissatisfaction with the schooling available to minority group children, especially poor minority group children, there is a curious lack of involvement as well as a lack of knowledge concerning these major social issues on the part of the beginning teachers studied here.

With few exceptions the teachers took an "it can't happen here" attitude. Either they felt that their particular school would not be affected or that their particular classroom would not be affected, or that something would happen to make the whole threat of a boycott disappear. There is also expressed by the teachers a lack of belief that the parents of their pupils could possibly be that concerned or involved in the improvement of their children's education to take action to change the schools.

Even those teachers who felt that some of their children might stay out of school gave no indication of careful understanding of the issues involved, and expressed great confusion concerning the aims of the boycott and its implications for the schools. It may be argued that some of this confusion was inevitable, for even the civil rights leaders could not predict in detail the implications for all classrooms. However, and this is perhaps the most serious of problems, there was little or no dialogue between black and white teachers, and little formal or informal discussion within schools to make for informed position-taking or, at the very least, informed citizenry.

The fear of exploring the problem of race relations and the problem of communication between black and white schoolteachers on this issue is highly revealing. It illustrates the reluctance of whites to acknowledge the reality of caste barriers in this country, and the difficulty black people have in communicating with white people they see as hostile and unwilling to understand. The very efforts of white teachers to be "color-blind," to see only children and not color, is often the result of a refusal to recognize that problems in race relations do exist and consciousness of the problem must precede solutions.

To the teacher who considers she is doing as good a job

as she can, a boycott threat by parents and outsiders appears as an unwarranted attack upon her own integrity. Concern for the children as individuals also causes teachers to be upset about the implications of school boycotts or school reorganization for young children. What the teachers do not see is that the massive educational failure evident in the *de facto* segregated schools of the inner city has profound implications for the future life chances of the minority groups attending them. The larger social and economic effect of educational retardation for Negroes and Puerto Ricans does not seem to be a major concern for the teachers. They see their pupils as individuals, and do not think in terms of the larger issues. That the children are not achieving they recognize, and this troubles them. They also complain about large classes, lack of help when needed, and early in their careers they express very serious concern for their own professional inadequacies. Yet they view parental and community action to reorganize, reorient, and gain assistance for the schools as a threat, rather than as an effort to improve schooling.

Like most educators, they view themselves as being committed to equal educational opportunity for all according to ability, and are shocked to have their schools and teaching accused of providing unequal opportunity for minority youth. Accustomed to placing the blame for pupil failure upon pupil inadequacy, lack of parental support, and community problems, it comes as a surprise to educators that even very poor parents are very much concerned about the failure of their children and believe that the cause of this failure rests with the schools themselves.

Since 1966, community pressures to improve the education of minority youth in the inner-city schools have moved from efforts to achieve integration to programs that emphasize local community control over the organization, staffing, and curriculum of schools situated within the urban ghetto. The shift in emphasis grew out of a recognition that desegregation was becoming an increasingly difficult goal within cities that were rapidly losing their white public school populations. In addition, the energies expended in boycotts seemed wasteful in the face of the counterpressures exerted by white groups. Results were not forthcoming. Recognizing the reality of *de facto* segregation, organized groups turned instead to a demand for increased local control over the schools their children were attending. The growth of black nationalism, the demands for Black Power, and a growing pride in race also contributed to the belief that non-integrated schools could provide a good education provided the schools were controlled by the local group and not by outsiders who were viewed as disinterested in the community.

In New York City, plans for decentralization of the schools to provide for increased community control were proposed in the McGeorge Bundy report.[2] Experimental school districts, financed by the Ford Foundation, were set up to work out plans for decentralization. Intermediate School 201 in Harlem and Ocean Hill-Brownsville drew national attention when parents demanded the right to participate in the choice of school principals and the right to hire and fire staff.

Many of the nation's large school systems have, as a result of the increasing recognition of the dangers inherent in racial separation made increasingly apparent by the growth of civil unrest, instituted human relations courses for teachers and administrators, in some instances making these courses mandatory. In addition, there is increased attention being paid to black history, ethnic traditions, and textbooks which recognize the existence of other than white people in this country. Also, sensitivity training for school staffs to develop awareness of interpersonal relations is witnessing a growing vogue. These programs are provided in-service as well as pre-service.

All of the above offer the promise of improving communication and understanding among people and are thus commendable. By themselves, however, they cannot attack the basic structural relationships that feed into antagonisms and distrust. If the school appears to be an intrusive, patronizing institution, controlled from the outside and maintaining social boundaries against the poor, and if the school continues to play a custodial role rather than an educative one, then conflict is likely to continue. The primary causes of the disputes will not be removed until inner-city children are achieving

---

[2] *Reconnection for Learning: A Community School System for New York City*, Mayor's Advisory Panel on Decentralization of the New York City Schools, 1967.

academically at as high a rate as children in other areas. Any program of school organization or curriculum which does not accomplish this will continue to be viewed as discriminatory and as maintaining minority children in lower-class positions in this country, for educational achievement is viewed as the path through which the children of the ghetto should be able to move in order to compete with the rest of America for the higher-status positions in the society.

To imbue education with the magical power to solve all social ills is to credit it with more than it can accomplish. On the other hand, it must be emphasized that the schools *do* play an increasingly significant role in the socialization of the young, and represent an institution through which the existing social order is maintained. It would appear at present that the schools are successful only in confirming the social status with which the children come in the first place, merely rubber-stamping a person with regard to his position in society. For most of those who are poor or in racial minority status, it has the effect of inducing school failure, second-class citizenship, sometimes overt hostility, acceptance of poverty, or early school-leaving. Those who are affluent are more likely to have reconfirmed their view that their position in society is theirs by virtue of birth—although we might add that the hippie movement has in effect been a "no thank you" expressed by the dissident children of the middle class, and recent college student unrest reflects growing discomfort at the obvious disparities in life chances presented the more affluent as opposed to the poor. What has compounded the problem for America is that the schools continue to teach the achievement ethos, the mass media encourage achievement and affluent consumption, our culture attributes social success to personal will, and yet these ideals are seriously discontinuous with the increasing fact of ascription of status by birth into a poverty or minority group.

In the United States, a compulsory education system has meant that those parents who are dissatisfied with the schooling provided their children by public systems must either move their residence to areas more compatible with or more responsive to parental interest, or must turn to private schooling. This has meant, however, that mainly those in the upper socioeconomic brackets have been able to exercise these options. The very poor, and members of minority groups who have faced discrimination in housing, are limited in their choice of residence, options for private schooling, and influence over school policy. Pious talk concerning the democratic nature of the public school system does not change the fact that for many it is unsatisfactory and social class has a great deal to do about the choices open to a family to do something about the situation. Movement to the suburbs or into private school systems are not choices readily available to the urban poor. At present a major alternative open to this group, when consciously dissatisfied with the schools, is to engage in social protest, a phenomenon all American inner-city school systems have seen develop in recent years.

Much of this social protest has centered on the eradication of *de jure* and *de facto* school segregation. More recent efforts have concentrated on decentralization of city school systems and the substitution of local community control. It would appear that even were local school districts under the direct control of local parent and community groups, this form of organization would not preclude the disaffection of some groups from what would remain essentially a monopolistic, compulsory education system. Such programs run the risk of being stillborn, strangled not only by the opposition of conservative forces supporting the traditional system, but also by internal factional disputes.

The most outspoken opponents to control over the schools by the ghetto community have been the educators themselves through their teacher and supervisory organizations. Although willing to support compensatory education programs, they have been unwilling to accept the local community as a controlling factor in school policy. Yet it is perhaps in establishing new structural relationships which permit the previously powerless to participate in establishing education policy, selecting teachers and administrators, deciding on locations of schools, and establishing standards of accountability that will best operate to improve the relationship between the residents of the inner city and the educational institutions attempting to serve them. This restructuring appears to be fundamental to the development of mutual respect essential for educational progress.

Teachers and their supervisors working in situations affected by major social and political issues such as school integration or community control are frequently troubled by the conflict they see between professional concerns and political decisions over which they have no control. Although teachers and principals of schools play a crucial role in the implementation of policy once it is established, they generally have within their individual positions very little if any control over the establishment of policy.[3] School principals are required to respond to directives from the headquarters above them without having the power to demand decisions based on their definition of the specific educational needs of their schools, and these directives frequently represent a vacillating role played by Boards of Education responding to the pressures of those forces in the community exerting the greatest strength at a given time. The teacher stands in an even greater position of powerlessness as regards problems affecting her class as a result of changes in school policy.

It is only through their own supervisory and teacher organizations that they are in a position to make their opinions known, and as political controversy and community power have developed, so have the supervisors and teachers countered with their organizational strength. Thus it is that a major effect of the political controversies centered about schools has been organizational efforts on the part of supervisors and teachers to exert their influence over school policy, to remove themselves from a position of powerlessness, and, most important, to protect their own interests. Competition among the various forces seeking to exert control over school policy is likely to continue.

Meanwhile, solution of the problem of educational failure in the inner city remains a primary issue. It is no longer tolerable for teachers in ghetto schools to be as uncommunicative or as uninformed as these beginning teachers appeared to be in 1964.

---

[3] See Robert A. Dentler et al. ed., *The Urban R's,* New York, Center for Urban Education, 1967.

POSTSCRIPT

As they moved through their first semester, the beginning teachers experienced emotions ranging from a state of euphoria to panic, exhilaration and disappointment, restiveness and calm acceptance of their new positions. In the process, the beginning teacher underwent a period of induction by the employing school, which exerts a powerful influence on her accommodation to a bureaucratic system, sometimes resulting in the abandoning of the lessons of her own pre-service education.

There would be no quarrel with shaping of the teacher by the school if the public schools of American inner cities were functioning effectively to prepare poor and minority group children for roles in a technological society in which the barriers of race, class, and sex no longer function to frustrate the social goals of equality of opportunity. But the schools of America's inner cities are not carrying out this function. They are not meeting the needs of the populations they serve, i.e., to prepare most for more than the lowest levels in the corporate structure of the larger society, and have become instead containers for the restive young and their sorely harassed keepers, providing not only little in the way of warmth and humaneness, but also frustration for those concerned with meeting the requirements of the new America. If teachers, as they are inducted by the employing school, are prepared to function as effective civil servants within an ineffective system, and are helped to accept the ongoing situation —something made increasingly easy by facile rationalizations concerning the inherent uneducability of disadvantaged, "deprived" children—then certainly this kind of teaching is useful only in perpetuating an archaic system.

At the same time, those directly engaged in the educational enterprise within schools, the supervisors, administrators, and the teachers themselves, do not enjoy the educational failure in their schools, and frequently blame poor or inadequate teacher preparation, as provided by the colleges, as a major cause for it. Dissatisfaction expressed by supervisory personnel concerning the preparation of teachers by the colleges is not uncommon, and the notion persists that somehow the teacher ought to arrive completely capable and in need of minimum assistance. Colleges in turn have not always been pleased with the reception accorded their students in the schools, especially during their pre-service training. Who should assume the blame for ineffective teaching, who should assume the responsibility for the preparation of teachers is argued frequently. This is not a very fruitful kind of argument. It does not take into account that no matter what kinds of strengths the pre-service training provides, the teacher is ordinarily abandoned by his or her college when graduated, and is then incorporated into the institution of the school where employed, and claimed for particular roles. The teacher education institution will graduate the student, but then what happens? Too frequently the teacher is claimed by those who basically have no respect for the poor and their children, who accept rationalizations for the failure of the institution to achieve ideal goals, and who operate as bureaucratic functionaries rather than as educators. Thus, the claiming institution, the school in which the teacher actually works, has a responsibility to be aware of its function to provide the beginning teacher with a constructive educational milieu in which to develop professional competence.

How then can teachers be best prepared to maintain high professional standards and to avoid degrading, frightening, and disillusioning experiences that portend no good for either themselves or the children entrusted to them?

The preparation of teachers should include, in addition to the necessary curriculum methods and psychology of child development, a perceptual framework contributed by the social sciences for an understanding of the social processes at work affecting the teacher and the children in the classroom, the social processes at work within the school, and the school and education within the context of the social forces of the larger society. Preparing the teacher to observe and interpret behavioral cues, to be conscious of the cultural context of behavior, and to understand her own role in the cultural process of socialization promises to be very supportive and useful. Equally important, the education of those in positions of leadership within schools, the supervisors and administrators, requires the development of understanding of social process in order to help teachers assume constructive roles. The institution of the school has its own traditions, and these are different for slum schools than they are for suburban schools; different for the so-called "better" classes on the grade than for the "slow" classes. Formal and informal structures exist within schools and influence the teachers and the children, all of whom are operating within the framework of a larger cultural system. This must be understood by all concerned with educational improvement, and all educators should make a conscious effort to see these processes at work.

In addition, those concerned with the preparation of teachers need to recognize that only with strong and consistent support from the teacher education institution during the beginner's period of induction into her position as teacher can those who enter schools in the ghettos and slums translate and stabilize their ideals into practices which can contribute to the revitalization of education for the children of the inner city.

The professional experiences of beginning teachers document the impact of the employing school on the opinions, practices, and satisfaction or dissatisfaction of new teachers and have important implications for teacher education programs. The power of the employing school, its bureaucratic structure and procedures, and the status system among teachers—based primarily upon tenure—tend to cause the neophyte teacher to modify and in some instances to abandon whatever she has been taught during her pre-service education. For this reason, the teacher education institution which hopes that its graduates will realize in their teaching practices the principles, attitudes, and methods it advocates must be prepared to invest a major portion of its expertise and efforts in intensive programs for new teachers *in service*.

Supervised teaching experience within inner-city schools is increasingly in vogue among teacher education institutions and mark a desire to provide realistic experiences for students. However, this generally takes place at the undergraduate level, and when actually assigned to a teaching position the student is no longer a responsibility of the college. The evidence points strongly, however, to the serious need for professional help during the initial teaching experience. Internship programs which offer professional assistance directly related to the teachers' ongoing experiences are useful, provided attention is paid to the induction of teachers by those with positive, constructive approaches. Workshops and consultative services should be available at or close to the teacher's place of employment.

All too often, beginning teachers, seeking to further their education, are enrolled in master's degree programs during their first year of teaching, and even though these are education programs, they are frequently discontinuous with the daily, on-the-job concerns of the teacher, and lead to both physical and emotional fatigue. A difficult day in the classroom needs analysis. Courses taken at a distant university at night, unrelated to the next day's time with the children, can prove unsatisfactory for all concerned.

Occasionally a person with charisma, a "natural," appears and is a great teacher. Most, however, are not charismatic. Becoming a teacher is an enormously complex process, often starting with one's first experience in kindergarten and extending through induction on one's first teaching job. Changes in the preparation of teachers are not as likely to effect significant changes in the education of inner-city school children as changes in the institutional framework within which the teacher must operate. Nonetheless, improved preparation and help will strengthen the resolve to work for improved professional standards, increased respect for the parents and their children, and the maintenance of one's own integrity and dignity in the face of serious social problems.

INDEX

Acculturation, 32–33 ff.
Adjusting, 141–211
Administration, 79–95. *See also* specific members
  and forbidden objects, theft, 128–30
  getting help from, 164–77. *See also* specific members, problems
  and rexograph machine, 79–83 ff.
Age, 40, 41
  and grouping, 103
Agrarian Socialism, 111 n
Agricultural peoples, 155, 190
"Alberto," 177
American Anthropologist, 120 n
American Journal of Sociology, 134 n
"Anita," 63, 64, 66
"Anita R.," 176, 178
"Anthropological View of Social System and Learning, An," 94 n
Anthropology, x–xii. *See also* specific theories
"Anthropology and Education: An Overview," xi n
Arensberg, Conrad M., 21 n
Art, 30–31, 82, 96–98 ff.
Assembly, 113–14 ff., 197
Assistant principals, 114–15 ff., 148, 149, 175, 176
  and cigarettes, 125
  and machismo, 28–29 ff., 35–36
  and observations, 143–44
  and shakedowns, frisking, 127
Attendance officers, 135
Ausubel, D., 25 n
Ausubel, Pearl, 25 n
Authority, establishing, 13–14. *See also* specific situations
Avoidance rituals, 121

Beal, Ralph L., 43 n
Becker, Howard S., 53, 107 n, 134 n
Behavior problems (discipline), 170–71
  and bypassing of teachers, 96–98 ff.
  and Christmas parties, 186–88, 190, 195
  and culture shock, panic, 17–20 ff.
  "dumping ground" and, 60–72
  first day, 11, 12
  and forbidden objects, theft, 124–30
  and machismo, 27–30 ff.
  and obscenity, 46–59, 67 ff.
  and observations, 151–52

Behavioral Science and Guidance . . ., 94 n
Bender, Mrs. Janet, 64–68 ff., 166–67
and boycott, 200–1
and Christmas, 189–90 ff.
and culture shock, 17–21, 24–26
and lesson plan, 73–76
and parents, 131–33 ff.
Benedict, Ruth, 36 n
Blau, Peter, 110 n
Boards of Education, 211
"Bobby," 17–19, 24
Bower, Miss, 185–86
and boycott, 203–4
Boycott, 199–216
discussion, 205–16
Brewster, Miss, 9–10, 125
Bronx High School of Science, 104
Brown, B. Frank, 109 n
Brown, Lawrence, 60–63, 69–70
Bundy, McGeorge, 208
Bureaucracy, 93–94, 110–11
Bussing, 203, 204, 205
Bypassing of teachers, 96–101
discussion, 99–101

Callahan, Raymond S., 83, 84 n
"Career of the Chicago Public School Teacher, The," 134 n
Cedar, Miss, 46–52 ff.
and boycott, 199–200
Ceremonies. *See* Rituals
Changes in Self and Racial Attitudes of Negro Children . . ., 25 n
Chapple, Eliot D., 155 n, 191 n
Christmas party, 185–98
Cigarettes, 124–25, 126, 129
Civil rights movement, 106. *See also* Boycott; Negroes
Clark, Kenneth B., 25 n, 118 n
Clark, Mamie P., 25 n
Cognitive style, 37
Colleges, 157, 214

"Concept of Culture, The," 39 n
Conflict, 86 n
Consultants, 169. *See also* specific situations
"Continuities and Discontinuities in Cultural Conditioning," 36 n
Coon, Carleton S., 155 n, 191 n
Co-ordinators, 168, 169
CORE, 200
Coser, Lewis, 111 n
Crawford, Mrs., 149
Cross, Dr., 166–67
Cultural anthropology, x–xii
Culture; and ethnocentrism, 39–40 ff.
Culture change, 32–33 ff.
Culture conflict, 27–37
discussion, 31–37
Culture shock, 17–26, 99
discussion, 21–26

Dark Ghetto, 118 n
Deans, and shakedowns, frisking, 127, 129
Decentralization, 208, 210
Demeanor, 121–22
Dentler, Robert A., 211 n
De Pauw, Mrs., 116
Devans, Miss, 38–39 ff., 97–98 ff., 204
DeVito, Mr., 125
Dewey, John, 84
Dickson, W. J., 84
"Dirty Dozens, the," 56–57
Discipline. *See* Behavior problems
Downstate Medical Center, 37 n
Doyle, Miss, 165
"Dozens, the," 56–57
Dufay, Frank R., 109 n
Dumping ground, classroom as, 60–72, 105
Dynamics of Bureaucracy, 110 n

Eddy, Elizabeth, 135 n

Index

Edmunson, Munio, 34 n
Education and the Cult of Efficiency (Callahan), 83, 84 n
Education and Culture, xi n
Education in Depressed Areas, 25 n
Education and the New America, 134 n
Effects of Ability Grouping, The, 104 n
"Ego Development Among Segregated Negro Children," 25 n
"Enculturation," 179–80
Escalator, the, 38–45
  discussion, 39–45
Ethnocentrism, 39–40 ff.
Etzioni, Amitai, 84 nff., 168 n
Euphoria, 1–14
  discussion, 13–14
Expectation, teacher, 105 ff.
"Experimental Study of Leadership and Group Life, An," 84 n
Exploitation, 113–23
  discussion, 117–23

"Fall," the, 16–76
Fatigue. *See also* Culture shock and lesson plan, 73–76
Fire drills, 6, 8
First day, 3–14
  discussion, 13–14
Forbidden objects, 124–25 ff.
Ford Foundation, 208
"Formal Education in an American Indian Community," 43 n
Frank, Miss (co-ordinator), 62, 79 ff., 89 ff.
Franseth, Jane, 104 n
"Freddy," 63–68
Fridays, 192
Frisking, 127, 128–30
Frost, Dr., 63 ff., 173–74 ff.
Fuchs, Estelle, 57 n, 107 n, 138 n, 205 n

Functions of Social Conflict, The, 111 n

Glee club, 114 ff.
Goffman, Erving, 120, 121
Goldberg, Miriam, 104 n
Gould, Bernice, 97
Gould, Miss Lucy, 102–3, 113–17 ff.
Grade 1/5, 133 ff., 200
  as dumping ground, 60–63, 69–70
  saga of, 172–84
Grade 2/6, 11–13, 14, 79–83, 202–3
  observation of, 151–53
Grade 2/3, 9–10, 125
Grade 2/4, 3–4, 143–46, 164–65
Grade 3/2, 38–45, 96–101, 204
Grade 3/4, 4–7, 205
Grade 3/5, 185–86, 203–4
Grade 4/2, 7–9, 46–52 ff., 149–51, 165–66, 199–200
Grade 4/3, 146–49, 153–54, 188–89
Grade 5/2, 63–68 ff., 166–67, 200–1
  and Christmas, 189–90 ff.
  and culture shock, 17–21, 24–26
  and lesson plan, 73–76
  and parents, 131–33 ff.
Grade 5/3, 102–3, 113–17
Grade 6/3, 27–37, 124–25, 186–88 ff., 201–2
Grammar, 44
Gross, Neal, 89–90
Grouping, 102–12
  discussion, 103–12
Guidance counselors, 63 ff.
  and culture shock, 17 ff.
  and shakedowns, frisking, 127, 129
  and speech problems, 60–61, 63

Hanes, Miss, 4–7, 205
Harlem, 208

Harris, Miss, 11–13, 14
  and boycott, 202
  and observation, 151–53
  and rexograph, 79–83 ff.
Hartley, E. L., 84 n
Havighurst, Robert J., 107 n
"Help!," 77–140
Help, obtaining, 164–71
  discussion, 167–71
Henle, Paul, 44 n
Herriot, Robert E., 89–90
Herskovitz, Melville J., 179 n
Hippies, 209
Hoijer, Harry, 43 n
Homans, George C., 118 n, 170 n
Honeymoon period, 1–14
  discussion, 13–14
Human Group, The, 118 n, 170 n
Human relations school of administration, 84–86
Hunter College, ix

Immigrants, 32. *See also* Puerto Ricans
Indians, American, 42–43
Industrial research, 94
Integration, 106–7. *See also* Boycotts
Intermediate School, 201, 208
Internship programs, 216
Interviews, 150–51
Introducing Social Change . . . , 21 n
Introduction to Anthropology, An, 43 n

Jacobson, Lenore, 105 n, 108 n
James, Mr., 47–48 ff.
"James B.," 200
"Jean," 19–20, 24–26
"Jimmy," 27–37
Johnson, David W., 25 n
Jones, Mrs., 172–73
"José," 187
"Joseph C.," 178
"Joseph R.," 176

Journal of Educational Sociology, 53 n, 107 n, 118 n
"Juan," 132
Julian, Mr., 165–66, 171

Kardiner, Abram, 25 n
Kelly, William, 39 n
Kimball, Solon, 94, 134 n, 156–57
Kluckhohn, Clyde, 39 n
Kooper, Miss, 27–31 ff., 124–25, 186–88 ff.
  and boycott, 201–2

Language, 43–44, 79 ff., 97, 100, 173. *See also* Spanish speaking
  obscenity, 46–59, 67 ff.
  parents and class barriers, 135–36
Language arts, 164–65. *See also* Reading
"Language, Thought and Culture," 44 n
Language, Thought and Culture, 44 n
Law, 87
Lee, Mr., 166–67
Lesson plans, 73–76
  discussion, 74–76
Lewin, Kurt, 84
Licensing, 157, 158
"Linda," 132
Linton, Ralph, 32 n, 33 n, 39 n
Lippitt, R., 84, 85 n
Lipset, Seymour M., 111 n
Lloyd-Jones, Esther, 94 n
Long, Mr., 96–98 ff.
Lost Generations, The, 25 n
Louis, Mr. (assistant principal), 114–15 ff.
Lunch, 7, 10, 131, 154
"Lydia A.," 176

McClellan, James E., 134 n
Machismo, 27–37
  discussion, 31–37
Macoby, Eleanor E., 25 n
Man and His Works, 179 n

Index

Management and the Worker, 84 n
Manitos . . . , Los, 34 n
Mark of Oppression . . . , The, 25 n
Marriage, xii–xiii, 155–56
Masculinity
  and the "Dozens," 56–57
  machismo, 27–37
Master teachers, 23, 169
Mayo, Elton, 84
Medical examinations, 126
Medicine, 87
Mental disturbance, 60–63 ff.
Merton, Robert K., 110 n
Middle class, 134–35
  and grouping, 107, 108
  hippies, 209
Modern Organizations (Etzioni), 84 nff., 168 n
Moore, G. Alexander, 106 n, 118 n
Moral behavior, 53 ff. *See also* Obscenity
More Effective School Program, 109

NAACP, 200–1
Names, 8
  teachers' first, 115, 120
"Nature of Deference and Demeanor, The," 120 n
Negroes (blacks), and race relations, 19–20, 24–26, 111, 169
  and boycott, 199 ff.
  and the "Dozens," 56–57
  and grouping, 106–7, 108
  and shakedowns, 130
Neugarten, Bernice L., 107 n
New admissions, 4–5
Newcomb, T. M., 84 n
New York City, 109, 205, 208. *See also* specific classes, situations
Niehoff, Arthur H., 21 n
"Non-Graded High School, The," 109 n
Norms, 118 ff., 170

Norris, Rita, 187–88
Numbers, grades and class, 3 n

Obscenity, 46–59, 67 ff.
  discussion, 52–59
Observations, 143–63
  discussion, 154–63
Ocean Hill-Brownsville, 208
Open School Week, 132–33, 136, 137
Oral reports, 132
Oveysey, Lionel, 25 n

Padilla, Elena, 34 n, 137 n
Panic, 16–76
Parents, 131–40
  discussion, 133–40
  and obscenity problem, 48–49, 58
Parker, Mrs. (assistant principal), 143–44 ff., 145
Parsons, Mrs., 175, 176
Passow, A. Harry, 25 n
"Pedro," 132
People of the Sierra, The, 34 n
Peters, Miss, 146–49, 153–54, 188–89
Phi Delta Kappan, 109 n
Phonetics, 173
Physical problems, 60–63, 69–70
Physicians, 87
Pickets at the Gates, 57 n, 107 n, 138 n, 205 n
Pitt-Revers, Julian, 34 n
Pizarre, Carlos, 65–66
"Playing the Dozens," 56–57
Plays, 131–32
Preparation, first day, 5
Presentation rituals, 121
Primitive Culture, 39 n
Principals, 89–90 ff., 211
  and bypassing of teachers, 96–97, 98 ff.
  and culture shock, 18–19, 23–24
  and "dumping ground," 63 ff.
  and exploitation, 114 ff.

Principals (cont'd)
getting help from, 165–66 ff.
See also specific situations
and grouping, 102–3 ff., 109–10 ff.
and lesson plans, 73, 74
and obscenity, 47–48 ff.
and observations, 144 ff.
and parents, 131–32
and rexograph, 81 ff.
and saga of Class 1/5, 173–74 ff.
and shakedowns, frisking, 127, 129, 130
Principles of Anthropology, 155 n, 191 n
Private world, 133, 134
Professionalism, 87 ff.
Project TRUE, ix, 106 n
Psychiatry, 36 n
Public world, 134
Puerto Ricans, 20. See also Spanish speaking; specific classes
and boycott, 199 ff.
and silence, 54
Pygmalion in the Classroom (Rosenthal and Jacobson), 105 n–6 n, 108 n

Questions, 152
Quizmo, 146–47

Race relations. See Negroes
"Racial Identification and Preference in Negro Children," 25 n
"Rascals," 33–34, 36
Reader in Bureaucracy, 110 n
Reading, 172–73. See also Language; Language arts
observation of, 143–46 ff.
remedial, 166–67
Readings in Social Psychology (Lippitt and White), 25 n, 84 n, 85 n
Realities of the Urban Classroom, 106 n, 118 n

Reconnection for Learning . . . , 208 n
Records,
anecdotal, 61, 70
reading of, 65–66, 71
Recruitment, teacher, xiii
Reid, Mr., 149–51
Religion, 191–92, 193
Remedial reading, 166–67
"Research in Grouping: A Review," 104 n
Rexograph machine, 79–95
discussion, 83–95
Rites of intensification, 185–98
Rites de passage, 143–63, 191
Rites of Passage, The (Van Gennep), 155 n, 156 n, 162 n, 191
Rituals, 143–63, 185–98
"Robert G.," 178
"Robert M.," 176–77
"Roberta," 132
Roethlisberger, F. J., 84
"Roger," 46–51 ff.
Rogers, Mrs., 17, 18, 63 ff.
Rogers, David, 25 n
Roman, Mrs., 73–74
Rosenthal, Robert, 105 n, 108 n
Roth, Miss, 96–98 ff.
Routines, 5, 8
Ryan, Mrs., 151–53

Samson, Miss, 7–9, 149–51, 165–66
Sapir-Whorfian hypothesis, 43
School Life, 104 n
Science of Man in the World Crisis, 39 n
Scientific management, 83–84, 90
Scientific Management, 83 n
Seabold, Miss, 60–63, 69–70 ff., 133, 200
and saga of Class 1/5, 172–84
Secretaries, school, 102
"Segregated Schools in New York City," 118 n

Index

Segregation, 106–7. *See also* Negroes
Sex; the sexes, 36–37, 71–72. *See also* Obscenity
 and administrative jobs, 89–90
 and the "Dozens," 56–57
 and grouping, 103
 and machismo, 27–37
 and shakedowns, frisking, 128
 Spanish vs. American attitudes, 33–34. *See also* Machismo
Shakedowns, 127, 129–30
Shouting, culture shock and, 21
Silence, 54–55
Simmel, George, 86 n
Size, class, 4, 72
Smith, Miss, 116
Soap, for obscene language, 52
"Social Class Variation in the Teacher-Pupil Relationship," 53 n, 107 n
Social classes
 and grouping, 107, 108
 and obscenity, 53
 parents and, 134–35 ff.
"Socialization," 179
Social Problems, 43 n
Social science theory, x
Society and Education, 107 n
Sociology of Teaching, The, 41 n
Spanish speaking, 97, 100, 199. *See also* Puerto Ricans
 machismo, 27–37
Specialists, 168, 169–70. *See also* specific jobs
Speech problems, 60–63, 69–70
Spindler, George, x–xi
Staff Leadership in Public Schools . . ., 90 n
Stark, Mr. (assistant principal), 28–29 ff., 35–36
Status, 209. *See also* Social classes
 and exploitation, 117 ff.
 rituals and, 154 ff.

Stealing, 125–30
Student teachers, 22
Study of Man, The, 32 n, 33 n
Subcultures, 41. *See also* specific groups
Substitute teaching, 7, 12, 14, 105, 168
Supervisors, 24, 165, 169. *See also* specific jobs
 and ritual, 159–60
Swanson, C. E., 84 n

Taylor, Frederick W., 83 n
Teacher trainers, 62, 73–74
Tenure, 158
Tests, 136
 and grouping, 103, 104–5, 107
Thanksgiving, 191–92, 193
Theft, 125–30
Think and Do, 164–65
"Thomas," 187
Time, teaching of, 146–47
"Tom," 51–52
Tracking, 107–8
Trent, Mr., 144, 145
Turnover, teacher, xii–xiii
Tylor, E. B., 39 n

Ungraded schools, 109
Ungrading the Elementary School, 109 n
Up from Puerto Rico, 34 n, 137 n
Urban R's, The, 211 n

"Vacuum Ideology," 42–43
Van Gennep, Arnold, 155, 156 n, 162, 191
Vocabulary, 44, 100. *See also* Language

Walk the White Line, 135 n
Waller, Willard, 41
Washington, D.C., 108 n
Watkins, William, 124
Wax, Murray L., 42–43
Wax, Rosalie H., 42–43
Weapons, 126 ff.

Westervelt, Esther M., 94 n
White, R. K., 84, 85 n
Whorf, B. L., 43 n, 44
"William," 132
Winters, Miss, 3–4, 143–46, 164–65, 202–3
Witkin, H., 37 n
Wolff, Kurt H., 86 n

Work assignments, exploitation and, 113–23
  discussion, 117–23
Working class. *See also* Social classes
  and grouping, 108
Writing, 12, 30, 31

ANCHOR BOOKS

AMERICAN HISTORY AND STUDIES

AMERICAN HUMOR—Constance Rourke, A12
AMERICAN LIFE IN THE 1840s—Carl Bode, ed., AD4
THE AMERICAN LITERARY REVOLUTION 1783–1837—Robert E. Spiller, ed., AD6
THE AMERICAN NOVEL AND ITS TRADITION—Richard Chase, A116
AMERICAN POETRY AND POETICS—Daniel Hoffman, ed., A304
THE AMERICAN PURITANS: THEIR PROSE AND POETRY—Perry Miller, ed., A80
AMERICAN RACE RELATIONS TODAY—Earl Raab, ed., A318
AMERICAN SOCIAL PATTERNS—William Petersen, A86
AMERICAN STRATEGY: A New Perspective—The Growth of Politico-Military Thinking in the United States—Urs Schwarz, A587
THE AMERICAN TRANSCENDENTALISTS: THEIR PROSE AND POETRY—Perry Miller, ed., A119
CAN AMERICAN DEMOCRACY SURVIVE COLD WAR?—Harry Howe Ransom, A402
CASTE AND CLASS IN A SOUTHERN TOWN—John Dollard, A95
CAVALIER AND YANKEE: The Old South and American National Character—William R. Taylor, A351
CHRISTIAN SCIENCE: Its Encounter with American Culture—Robert Peel, A446
THE CIVIL WAR IN AMERICA—Alan Barker, A274
THE COMPLETE POEMS AND SELECTED LETTERS AND PROSE OF HART CRANE—edited with an Introduction and Notes by Brom Weber, A537
THE CONGRESSMAN—Charles L. Clapp, A426
CONSTRAINT AND VARIETY IN AMERICAN EDUCATION—David Riesman, A135
THE DEATH PENALTY IN AMERICA, Revised Edition—Hugo Adam Bedau, ed., A387
THE EMANCIPATION PROCLAMATION—John Hope Franklin, A459
THE EXPLODING METROPOLIS—the Editors of Fortune, A146
THE FEDERALIST PAPERS, Second Edition—Roy P. Fairfield, ed., A239

American History and Studies (continued)

THE FIRST AMENDMENT: The History of Religious Freedom in America—William H. Marnell, A472

THE FIRST NEW NATION—The United States in Historical and Comparative Perspective—Seymour Martin Lipset, A597

IDEOLOGY AND POWER IN THE AGE OF JACKSON—Edwin C. Rozwenc, ed., AD1

THE IMMEDIATE EXPERIENCE—Robert Warshaw, A410

THE INDIAN AND THE WHITE MAN—Wilcomb E. Washburn, ed., AD2

KILLERS OF THE DREAM—Lillian Smith, A339

LITERATURE AND THE AMERICAN TRADITION—Leon Howard, A329

MAN-MADE MORALS: Four Philosophies That Shaped America—William H. Marnell, A613

MARGARET FULLER: AMERICAN ROMANTIC, A Selection from Her Writings and Correspondence—Perry Miller, ed., A356

THE NATURE OF PREJUDICE—Gordon Allport, A149

THE NEGRO AND THE AMERICAN LABOR MOVEMENT—Julius Jacobson, ed., A495

ON NATIVE GROUNDS—Alfred Kazin, A69

THE ORGANIZATION MAN—William H. Whyte, Jr., A117

POLITICS IN AMERICA—D. W. Brogan, A198

POPULAR CULTURE AND INDUSTRIALISM, 1865-1890—ed. by Henry Nash Smith, AD5

THE POSITIVE THINKERS: A Study of the American Quest for Health, Wealth and Personal Power from Mary Baker Eddy to Norman Vincent Peale—Donald Meyer, A525

PROTESTANT, CATHOLIC, JEW—Will Herberg, A195

PURITAN VILLAGE: The Formation of a New England Town—Summer Chilton Powell, A441

QUEST FOR AMERICA—Charles Sanford, ed., AD3

RACE AND NATIONALITY IN AMERICAN LIFE—Oscar Handlin, A110

RELIGIOUS CONFLICT IN AMERICA—Earl Raab, ed., A392

TEACHER IN AMERICA—Jacques Barzun, A25

THE THEOLOGY OF JONATHAN EDWARDS—Conrad Cherry, Introduction by Will Herberg, A542

WHITE MAN, LISTEN!—Richard Wright, A414

WHO DESIGNS AMERICA?—ed. by Laurence B. Holland, A523